GET YOUR
ASSETS
IN GEAR!

Smart Money Strategies

JAN DAHLIN GEIGER, CFP®, MBA

Outskirts Press, Inc.
Denver, Colorado

Get Your Assets in Gear!
Smart Money Strategies
All Rights Reserved
Copyright © 2008 Jan Dahlin Geiger, CFP®, MBA
V5.0 R1.0

Cover Image © 2008 JupiterImages Corporation
All Rights Reserved. Used With Permission.

Outskirts Press
http://www.outskirtspress.com

ISBN-13: 978-1-59800-935-4

Library of Congress Control Number: 2007925957

Outskirts Press and the "OP" logo are trademarks belonging to
Outskirts Press, Inc.

Printed in the United States of America

What Others Are Saying About *Get Your Assets in Gear!*

"This fast-moving, smart book shows you how to get your entire financial life organized, and achieve financial independence faster than you ever thought possible." – **Brian Tracy, Author, *The Way to Wealth***

"If you're ready to begin creating financial freedom, then read and apply the strategies in this brilliant book by Jan Geiger. They will transform your life!" – **James Malinchak, Two-Time College Speaker of the Year, Co-Author, *Chicken Soup for the Athlete's Soul*, Co-Author, *Chicken Soup for the College Soul***

"The key to financial success is starting early. Geiger's book is a fantastic roadmap for both young adults and parents who are trying to raise fiscally fit children. Her easygoing narrative makes the reading as pleasurable as spending a productive afternoon with a wise friend. My thumbs are up...way up." – **Bobbie D. Munroe, CFP®, Chairman**

Emeritus, **Financial Planning Association of GA, and Owner of Fraser Financial**

"Easy, fun, and practical, three words I never thought I would use in the same sentence as the word money. I can now because Jan does indeed make the topic of money fun again! This is a fantastic guide for those who are ready to know that they can have the financial future they REALLY want!" – **Doreen Banaszak, Author, Teacher, and Coach, www.your-life-is-now.com**

"Every parent who has attended Jan's Raising Money-Wise Kids workshops in our community has been inspired by her personal success and thrilled with her common-sense advice and insights for teaching kids about money. Her first book, Get Your Assets in Gear!, *is a wonderful money management guide that should be required reading for every young adult! Her easy approach to building wealth is something everyone can learn to live with—and live well!"* – **Lisa Malice, Ph.D., Youth Financial Literacy Program Coordinator**

"Jan has provided one of the most important keys to success in any long-term family financial plan: how to prevent a divorce later on by establishing a financial game plan even before you're married. And if you didn't get that advice soon enough, there's still time to recover—and she explains how." – **Bob Littell, CLU, ChFC, FLMI, SRM, President, Littell Consulting Services and Chief NetWeaver, Author of *The Heart and Art of NetWeaving***

"Absolutely everybody should take control of his or her financial future, and Jan's book is a great way to start. It is a wonderful reference for the broad range of topics involved." – **Rona Wells, President, Wells Holdings, Former President, National Association of Women Business Owners (NAWBO), Atlanta Chapter**

*"*Get Your Assets in Gear! *Financial independence and the attainment of financial freedom is a focused, goal-driven journey taken one step at a time. Jan Dahlin Geiger has laid out a common sense trail guide for young adults. 'Money-smart' wisdom born of experience is a priceless gift, delivered with*

clarity in this useful book. Buy it for yourself. Parents and grandparents, give it to your children. Starting early with a solid financial plan is the key to long run success!" – **Lewis J. Walker, CFP®, CIMC, CRC, Owner of Walker Capital Management Corp.**

"Financial whiz Jan Geiger has written a fabulous guide to financial freedom for young people. This is the book I wish I had read growing up. Filled with upbeat stories told in an engaging manner, it gives you all the basics from student loans to car loans to real estate. Follow your 'Money Mom's' simple recipes and you can relax knowing your financial future is assured!" – **Chellie Campbell, author of The Wealthy Spirit**

"Jan Geiger's book provides practical, usable advice. To her readers I would say: here is a plain recipe that anyone can use. Follow the recipe, and it will work—period." – **C. Andrew Millard, CFP®, author of Low-Stress Investing: 10 Simple Steps to a Worry-Free Portfolio**

Get Your Assets in Gear! provides a straightforward foundation to build your financial future by learning to handle your money in the right way." – **Hugh Massie, President and Founder of Financial DNA Resources, Inc. and Author of Financial DNA–Discovering Your Unique Financial Personality for a Quality Life**

"Jan explains personal finances with a simplicity that even tax attorneys and stock brokers would find beneficial. It's this expertise of hers and passion to help young people that made the Wedding Television Network seek her out to be our financial expert on our programs relating to wedding expenses and financial affairs of new marriages." – **Tim Ulmer, Vice President, Wedding Television Network**

This book is dedicated to my mother
Dr. Geraldine Dahlin
who taught me how to be fabulously financially fit.

Contents

Disclaimer

This book is designed to provide accurate and authoritative information regarding the subject matter covered. It is not intended as specific investment advice to any individual. This book is sold with the understanding that the author is not engaged in rendering legal, accounting, or other professional advice to you. If professional advice or other expert assistance is required, you should consult with a competent professional (see Chapter 11 for how to find an advisor).

Every effort has been made to make this book as complete and accurate as possible. However, there may be mistakes, both typographical and in content. Therefore, this should be used as a general guide and not as the ultimate source of information. All facts and figures provided are from sources the author believes to be reliable and are assumed to be correct, although accuracy cannot be guaranteed.

The purpose of this book is to educate, inspire, and entertain. The author and publisher shall have neither liability nor responsibility to any person or entity with respect to any loss or damage caused, or alleged to have been caused, directly or indirectly from this book.

Acknowledgements

I have numerous people to thank for making this book a reality. My first and most important thank you is to my wonderful husband, Jerry Geiger, who patiently accepted the many hours that I was glued to my computer writing. No one could ever ask for a more supportive and encouraging husband!

Brett and Blake Chalfant, my two sons, were my inspiration. They remained in mind as I wrote each chapter. Witnessing Blake and Brett applying the financial lessons they received from me is a great thrill. At the ripe old age of 23, Brett began teaching financial basics to the sailors on his ship, the USS Abraham Lincoln, CVN 72. Both of my sons are fabulous with their money and make me proud in countless other ways!

To my sister, Kimberly Dahlin Cain, I cannot express how much it has meant to have a consistently enthusiastic cheerleader on my team. Kim has always motivated me to become the person she already believes I am.

To my special friend, Essie Escobedo, owner of Office Angels, I thank not only for sending angel after angel to help me, but also for being the best encourager and most caring ally anyone could ever hope for.

To Joseph Dixon, my life coach and business coach, owner of On-the-Court Coaching. Joseph is constantly encouraging me to expand my horizons, and I am incredibly grateful and indebted for his powerful coaching over the last two years.

To the incredible people in my office at LongView Wealth Management, most especially my Staff Financial Planner, Scott Lewis, CFP®; my assistant, Stephanie Beckman; and the two men who really make it all happen, Wes Bigler, CFP® and Quinton Fisher.

To the dedicated and caring financial planners who read this book to ensure that the content is as correct as possible: Wes and Quinton from my office, as well as Chad Zimmerman, CFP®, Bobbie Munroe, CFP®, and Bonnie Hughes, CFP®.

To Brian Tracy, whose teachings have changed the course of my life and to Mark Victor Hansen, whose book marketing seminars inspire me to think smarter and on a larger scope.

Writers find inspiration from other writers. Some of my recent favorites are Chellie Campbell (*The Wealthy Spirit*), Esther and Jerry Hicks (*Ask and It is Given*), and Lynn Grabhorn (*Excuse Me, Your Life is Waiting*).

I want to thank the countless individuals who have come to my seminars over the last few years, especially those who have urged me to write this book to make a difference to a larger audience.

A big hug goes to my "Terrific Team Thirty," the thirty young volunteers who read the original manuscript of this book and offered invaluable feedback to make this book the best it could be.

I especially want to thank Alison Mondragon, who took the time to send me dozens of pages of detailed feedback and questions. If I have succeeded in addressing most of your questions, Ali gets a big portion of the credit.

I've been told that editing a book is the most important step of the entire process. I am so appreciative of not only a quality editing job, but also for all the encouragement I received from my two exceptionally talented editors, Shellie Hurrle of A-1 Editing Service, LLC and Sallie Boyles, owner of Write Lady, Inc.

I'm very grateful to the three fabulous friends who joined me in reading through the manuscript one final time, ensuring every last detail was correct: Judy Hamberg, Stacey Greenwald, and

Cecily Sapp.

I extend gratitude to my wonderful clients who make my career so rewarding and enjoyable. I am deeply grateful to them for entrusting me to help them achieve their financial dreams.

Introduction

Let's start by thinking of your financial planning in terms of baking a cake. Just as I'd advise you to make your first attempt with a cake mix, which requires that you add only eggs, oil, and water, I've written this book to give you the fastest and easiest formula for wealth. Once you've mastered these ideas, the day may come when you'd like more in-depth tools, like learning to bake from scratch—perhaps becoming a French pastry chef of money management! But for now, our recipe will be short and sweet. Getting started will be easy. In fact, think of this book as your deluxe starter mix.

The chapters are written in a similar manner to how I've always talked to my sons, Brett and Blake, who are in their early twenties. As a financial advisor, I had no greater goal with my sons than to provide them with the skills to achieve financially successful lives. Because they were young when I began their financial education, I quickly got in the habit of defining unfamiliar terms plainly and providing only enough information to get them going. Bottom line: I learned to capture their attention!

My methods worked. Both young men are financially independent; neither has come to their mother for a penny. Having also taught many seminars in the same way with success, I now share my process with you. While you can benefit from the advice in this book at any age, I'm hoping that you're picking it up as a young adult, when time and compound interest tip the scales heavily in your favor. If not, late is better than never, and I'm excited to get you up to speed.

Back in 1973, when I was 24, I read the book *The Richest Man in Babylon.* I knew then without equivocation that I was going to be rich. Everything the author talked about was so simple and easy to implement. Even though I was earning only $8,000 a year and had no delusions that my salary would soon skyrocket, I was disciplined and determined to avoid debt. I would also save a little money every month. That year I paid off the last of my college debts and began saving 10% of my income. And guess what? I found that the equation for becoming rich was almost as simple as staying out of debt and saving 10%! If only everyone my age had read that same book!

People in their forties and fifties who attend my seminars constantly ask, *"Why didn't I learn this when I was in my twenties?"* and *"Why didn't my parents teach me to do any of these things?"* Plain old fear is the main reason people fail to take financial action. Numbers are complicated and boring—or so people think. Haven't you procrastinated when you feared you wouldn't accomplish something well? Who wants to jump into an unfamiliar subject? Not me. Avoiding the dreaded job rather than attempting it (all the while fearing you'd do it poorly) is more comfortable. But a successful life is not about comfort.

Rather than scare you, however, I am going to erase your fears. And I'm willing to bet that any financial phobia that's been choking you will loosen its grasp the minute you start following my recommendations—especially when you see how quickly they empower you and your bottom line. I hope you're inspired by the fact that once you understand each "how-to", all you need is the right attitude to get your assets in gear!

My mother was the ultimate financial teacher and I, her willing student. Just as she taught me that baking a delicious cake was as straightforward as carefully measuring and mixing the right ingredients and baking the batter for the right amount of time, she showed me that financial independence was easily attainable with clear, specific, measurable goals—with time limits. I learned to follow such a "recipe" with directions that were surprisingly simple!

With this book, I hope to be that wise, nurturing voice in your life, no matter how old you are. Considering that fewer than 20 percent of people 65 or older are financially well off, we can logically assume that 80 percent of us don't learn how to handle our money well from our parents. This book is my way of giving back all that I've received from my mom.

I'd be delighted to hear from you with any thoughts, suggestions, or stories you'd like to share about your own delicious recipes—especially the ones that fatten your wallet rather than your waistline.

Here's to you!

Happy reading,

Jan Dahlin Geiger, CFP®, MBA
Atlanta, Georgia
May, 2007

Chapter 1

Is This Book for You?

Money isn't the most important thing in life, but it's reasonably close to oxygen on the "gotta have it" scale.

~ Zig Ziglar

F ew things upset me more than buying a book only to discover that it either rehashes everything I already know, or that the contents are so over my head that an advanced degree is necessary to implement the suggestions, much less understand them. The following chapters should be easy to understand, easy to execute, and—most of all—motivating! To help you find out if this book is for you, I have created a brief quiz.

Please take a moment to fill in your answers *honestly* next to today's date, disregarding the additional date columns for the moment. Check the questions for which your answer is *yes*. (Add a checkmark for all that don't apply to you, such as if you don't have children.)

1

	Question Check if Yes	8/28/08 Today's Date	Date	Date	Date	Date
1	Do you live in financial harmony with your partner (if you have one)? Specifically, are less than 1/3 of your disagreements about money?					
2	Do you pay your credit cards in full each month?					
3	Can you claim to have no debt other than a mortgage?					
4	Do you buy cars rather than lease them?	✓				
5	Do you save at least 10% of your income specifically for retirement?					
6	Do you save at least 3% of your income for each child's college education (if applicable), and did you start doing so when he or she was born? If so, is the money in a 529 plan?					
7	Do you have enough money in an emergency fund to get by for at least three months if you are sick, disabled, unemployed, or evacuated because of a hurricane or other natural disaster?					

	Question Check if Yes	Today's Date	Date	Date	Date	Date
8	Do you have adequate insurance for your car and home? How about life, disability, and health insurance?					
9	Do you have a will and/or a trust, a general or financial power of attorney, and a healthcare power of attorney?					
10	Do you believe that at your current rate of progress, one day you'll be financially set for life?					

Now, add up the total number of *yes* answers. If you answered in the affirmative 8 out of 10 times, your positive actions have already incorporated the information in this book. Congratulations! You're ready for that French pastry course! (Still, you might consider this book as a gift for friends or family in need of financial empowerment.)

If, however, you answered *no* to three or more of the questions, this book could be your best ally to help you get your financial house in order.

The second date column is the most exciting; there you'll be writing the date of one year from today. With that done, retrieve your PDA or calendar to make an appointment with yourself to pick up this book on that date to retake the quiz. I promise that you'll be *thrilled* to see all the progress you've made in one short year! (You'll see that I have provided several columns for scoring yourself over the years should you wish to perform a yearly appraisal.)

Reasons to Read this Book

I intend to answer many of your questions about money. In preparation, find out if any of these statements or questions resonates with you.

1. My parents always fought about money. Because money is one of the key factors in divorce, I want to learn how my partner and I can handle our finances correctly.

2. I've decided to be rich. What should I be doing right now to make sure that happens?

3. I'm drowning in debt and don't have a cushion in case of an emergency. How do I get out of debt and start saving money?

4. I've heard a great deal about budgets, but how do I learn to stop hating the idea and actually *want* to take action?

5. We're getting ready to buy our first house. How do we figure out how much we can afford? Are there tricks to finding a good mortgage?

6. I was recently turned down for a car loan because my credit score is too low. What components make up a credit score? How can I raise mine quickly?

7. Dad said that money was the root of all evil, but that view feels outdated and dangerous. How can I revise such engrained teaching and also ensure that I'll have enough money to live on when I retire?

8. Is it true that giving money away to charity will attract financial abundance, or is that just mystical mumbo jumbo?

9. I've worked hard, I no longer have debt, and I'm saving money every month. It's time to start investing, but I'm scared to death that I'll lose my savings. Is it safe to buy stocks, bonds, and mutual funds? If so, do I need to consider other investments? Most of all, how do I know whom to trust to guide me?

Not only will we discuss these and other important issues in-depth, but we'll also work on moving you quickly past any actions that will sabotage your success. Still, you might be questioning why everyone isn't doing what you're about to do to become rich if it's so easy. Good question! The simple answer is this: It's human nature to resist change. Too often, keeping our bad habits—even ones that cause major problems—is often easier than choosing to adopt new behaviors. Remember, therefore, to get back on the right track as quickly as possible if you happen to veer off course.

Despite all the cautions, thankfully, this information *is* as easy as I've promised. And, there's no time like the present to start!

Action Step 1: Take this quiz today, and then mark your calendar to take it again in a year to see how much progress you have made.

Chapter 2

Do You Need a Financial Attitude Adjustment?

If a person gets his attitude toward money straight, it will help straighten out almost every other area in his life.

~ Billy Graham

Childhood Lessons Are Powerful

What you learn about money as a child directly influences your feelings as an adult. Nevertheless, it's never too late to change your attitude toward money. In order to get rich, a positive attitude is critical! In fact, without the right attitude, you will never take action. That's why we are tackling this topic up front.

Let's start by defining the word *rich,* since it means something different from one person to another. When I use the word, I am referring to financial independence. No matter what type of career or professional path you choose, being rich is about saving enough money during your working lifetime to design *exactly* the kind of life that you want to have. At first, you work to earn your money; in time, your money works to earn an income for you.

Does this mean that the more you make, the less you will have to work and save? Absolutely not! Think about it: If you work in a job paying $30,000 a year, it will take far less savings to make you feel rich than it will for someone who is used to living on a $200,000 salary.

Let's consider your feelings about rich people. Ultimately, if you associate the rich with negative ideas, you will certainly never become one of them. Growing up, what did the people around you say about being wealthy?

- Rich people are greedy.
- Getting rich is too complicated and time-consuming.
- If you make too much money, you'll lose all your old friends.
- Rich people have to work too hard.
- Rich people don't care about the important things in life.
- Money is the root of all evil.
- Rich people usually raise selfish, spoiled children.
- Having to manage a great deal of money is extremely difficult and time-consuming.
- Even if you manage to save plenty of money, you're just going to lose it if you invest it.
- A little guy like me can't be successful with money when I have to compete with rich people and their expensive advisors.
- If I spend time on my investments, I won't have time for any fun in my life.

Thinking negatively about money will almost certainly guarantee that you will never accumulate wealth. You've probably heard that a person does nothing that is contrary to what is believed in the subconscious mind. Nowhere is this condition truer than with money.

> **If you associate the rich with negative ideas, you can be certain you will never be one of them.**

Rich People Think and Act Rich

Rich people typically become rich because of their mindsets (attitudes) and the result of how they apply their knowledge (actions). Such attitudes and actions last over a lifetime. Therefore, although a wealthy individual might lose his or her money, the person will often regain the loss (think Donald Trump, who nearly went broke but became a multimillionaire once again).

For instance, rich people generally believe that one *must* pay oneself first. They know how hard it is to save money, so for them, saving is never optional. After saving, they live on whatever is left and avoid using debt to finance excess spending.

In fact, the wealthy usually consider debt to be a dirty four-letter word. They believe that consumer debt is all about buying more than one can afford. Debt is simply negative savings. (We're not talking about business debt or mortgages here.)

Most wealthy people maintain the following attitudes:

- Money delivers freedom, fun, advantages, and choices.
- Money provides for better schooling and superior medical care.
- Money allows you to be more generous toward those in need.
- Money lets you do what you want with your life. You don't have to work doing something you don't love.
- Money provides security, allowing you to worry less and sleep better at night.
- Money allows you to travel the world and experience more of the pleasures in life.
- With money you can roll with the punches if a disaster should occur (e.g., a hurricane, the furnace dying, or the car conking out).

When I consider how strongly early teachings impact our adult beliefs and actions, I realize I am incredibly fortunate to have been raised by a mom who managed money fabulously. I often heard her say, "Money doesn't buy happiness, but I'd rather be rich and miserable than poor and miserable." Those words have played in my head my entire life, and all that I learned from her has supported my goal of being financially secure. No matter whether I'm wildly miserable or incredibly happy, I still want to be rich!

Even without the benefit of fiscally responsible parenting, you can empower yourself to become wealthy. Only 20 percent of the millionaires in this country inherited their wealth—the remaining 80 percent earned their wealth themselves. My attitude has always been: if they can do it, I can too. Always remember, a positive attitude is instrumental in achieving financial success!

> **Approximately 80% of the millionaires in this country earned their money rather than inheriting it.**

Choose to Change Your Thinking

When you are thinking about money, what do you feel? Are you excited that one day you'll be extremely well-off? Or do you carry a knot in your stomach and an urgent desire to change the subject? You can *decide* today that you will maintain a positive mental outlook that moves you toward your goals. Reject ideas and feelings that hold you back.

Easier said than done, right? Wrong. Put yourself on a 30-day mental attitude plan. Starting today, each time you catch yourself thinking a negative thought about money, say aloud to yourself, "No, I reject that thought!" Then write down the empowering thought you *choose* in its place to move toward your goal. Say that positive thought aloud. Say it repeatedly until you actually feel a positive physical change in your body.

> **Decide today that you will play only mental messages that move you toward your goals.**

As an example, suppose you catch yourself thinking that you'll never get out of debt—that you're just too far in the hole. Reject that thought immediately. Repeat the following to yourself several times: "I'm a smart person, and I can do this. Many others have prevailed over debt, and I will, too!" Keep repeating this until you truly feel it. And say the words as if you truly believe them; eventually, you will!

Do you resent that some of your friends are receiving financial assistance from their parents or grandparents, while you must achieve your financial goals completely on your own? If so, grasp the great opportunity to choose a positive mental attitude about this notion. Instead of being envious or feeling sorry for yourself, revel in the fact that you are becoming stronger and wiser than your friends. I have not met many people who became effective money managers when the "Bank of Mom and Dad" was financing all or part of their spending!

When you resolve to work on your mental attitude diligently for 30 straight days, you will create a new habit that moves you toward your goals. Don't believe me? After 30 days of applying this strategy, send me an email to let me know your results. I have challenged countless people with this exercise. Many have accepted my challenge, and all of them to date have reported success.

When you know the result will bring you that much closer to your financial goals, isn't it worth developing and practicing a new habit? You have everything to gain!

Positive Thinking Exercises

Volumes have been written and spoken about the impact that our thoughts have on our actions, and the concept is quite pertinent in learning how to become wealthy. If we focus our thoughts on our lack of money, thinking that we can't pay the bills, that we will never get free of debt or save money, then those are the exact conditions we will perpetuate.

11

To reverse the negative cycle, we can begin by thinking positive thoughts which empower positive actions regarding money. In the book *Ask and It Is Given* by Esther and Jerry Hicks, there are imaginative exercises that I often share with clients. As a form of calisthenics for the brain, one such exercise enables you to create a feeling of prosperity in your life. In your imagination, you will "spend" an increasing amount of money each day on anything you desire.

For example, let's suppose you give yourself $1,000 of imaginary money to "spend" on day one. Each day thereafter, you will increase the amount of your spending money by $1,000. Therefore, you will have $8,000 to spend on day eight and $47,000 to spend on day 47. By day 341, you will have $341,000 in your pretend pocket. If you continue, you will have "spent" over $66 million in the course of one year.

For an example, I'll let you take a peek at one of my actual journal entries during my own positive spending exercise:

Day 62: $62,000 to "spend"

- $20,000 toward my new house fund for my luxurious master bedroom closet, which comes complete with dressing room and plenty of storage
- $10,000 to feed AIDS orphans in Africa
- $10,000 for job retraining classes for people displaced by Hurricane Katrina
- $10,000 to the Murphy family to put toward the building fund for their new house
- $5,000 to Jeff, my brother, to have his book edited
- $5,000 to my friend Wendy for items for her new home
- $2,000 for two beautiful, custom-made red pantsuits

In all honesty, the exercise didn't affect me much in the early days because I could easily envision myself buying most everything on my list. Soon, however, I had to start "spending" bigger amounts to use up all the money, and figuring out where all the money would go definitely kicked me up a level in my thinking. By the time I reached day 50, I experienced tremendous excitement and motivation. I was "spending" money on things I had never dreamed of buying, and I loved the thrill of having the capacity to contribute to the many charitable causes that I believe in so passionately, even if only in my imagination.

I began to feel more prosperous, and, not surprisingly, I began to believe that I could earn more money in order to buy some of those "wants" in real life. And that is the purpose of the exercise. If you feel more prosperous, your thoughts will change, and you will begin to attract more money. The way it works is almost magical. Don't believe me? Try it for 90 days and then tell me about your results!

> **Positive thinking exercises can make you feel more prosperous; therefore, you'll create prosperity in your life.**

Many inspirational authors and speakers further encourage us to put our desires and dreams in writing. Start making your own lists. And as you list each aspiration, consider how you will feel when that dream becomes a reality. I love starting out my day with such reflections.

I have provided some ideas to fire up your imagination, but your list should reflect the goals that will have the most powerful effect on you.

- When I can repay my debt in large chunks every month, I will feel....
- When I cut up my credit cards and live well on a cash-only basis, I will feel....
- When I am offered a full scholarship, I will feel....
- When I soon receive a pay raise, I will feel....
- When I receive a sizeable bonus this year, I will feel....
- When I find the car that I need at an excellent price, I will feel....
- When I have my dishwasher repaired rather than having to buy a new one, I will feel....

- When I increase my contribution to my 401(k) plan, I will feel....
- When I find I can easily track my spending every day, I will feel....

This exercise is especially effective because it's realistic. Your mind will accept the conditions because each desire is within reach. Moreover, you will find that the more your mind dwells on these wonderful thoughts, the more you will attract each situation.

The Effects in My Own Family

My parents, who divorced when I was 22, provided excellent examples of what to do with money and what not to do. Even though my mother earned less than half of my father's salary, she followed all the principles in this book. Consequently, she was comfortable throughout her retirement, which began at the relatively early age of 62. During her last 16 years, I frequently heard her say that she had all the money she needed in order to do everything she wanted. When she died in 2002, she left a sizeable inheritance to my brother, sister, and me.

In contrast, my father violated some of the principles you will soon learn. Now 94, he resides in an assisted living facility, and my siblings and I pay a portion of his expenses. He will leave no inheritance. During the course of the last two decades, my dad has frequently complained about not having enough money to do what he wanted.

Again, my mother's example was fundamental to my writing this book. She filled my head with beliefs that continuously move me toward financial wellbeing. One of the most important beliefs she instilled in me was the necessity of staying out of debt. Her advice: "Don't do debt. If you can't pay cash, you can't afford it. Paying interest is like throwing money out the window."

She also advised me that buying on credit isn't a good idea because I could never presume to know my future income—or to assume it would even exist. Because my mother repeatedly stressed the value of remaining debt free, all the while impressing me with her positive beliefs about handling money, I have easily remained clear of debt and saved money every month since I was 24. And those actions have enabled me to accomplish what I have today.

> **Fill your head with beliefs that continuously move you toward financial wellbeing.**

Daily Affirmations

If you realize that you harbor numerous negative beliefs about money, consider reading a book that is completely focused on changing those beliefs into powerful, uplifting, encouraging thoughts. *The Wealthy Spirit* by Chellie Campbell is a favorite resource of mine that I have put to work for myself as well as for clients and friends to achieve positive outcomes. The book is arranged over 365 pages so that you can read one page a day. Each day ends with an affirmation for you to repeat in order to recondition your mind. Here are some examples:

- People love to give me money!
- I am rich and wonderful.
- I am now earning a large income doing what I love.
- Something wonderful is happening to me today—I can feel it!
- A lot more money is coming into my life.
- I am a money magnet!
- Money comes to me easily and effortlessly.
- I am a winner—winning often and winning big!
- I receive large sums of money, just for being me!

Select a few affirmations to repeat 10 or 20 times a day. While they may make you laugh aloud, I'll tell you from my personal experience that they also work. Say them and you will attract more money into your life.

My experience has shown that the most critical ingredient in becoming rich is a positive mental attitude. The following point is worth highlighting: *Whatever you believe is what you will attract more of in your life.* If your attitude is misguided, you are highly unlikely to take the right actions. And failing to act is sabotage. Therefore, don't read ahead until you have repeated such affirmations as this: "This is it! I will hit the eject button from now on if I catch myself thinking negative, limiting thoughts about money!"

Whatever you believe is what you will attract more of in your life.

If you get your assets in gear with a positive attitude, you will soon realize that getting rich is easy!

Take Specific Action Now

Review the examples of negative thinking in the first column, adding your own at the bottom. Then, in the next column, write an opposing affirmation that will help you begin retraining your mind.

Negative Thinking	Positive Thinking
I can never save money.	I am saving money now and can add more with each pay raise.
I just can't pay off my debt.	I am paying off my debts steadily each month.
I can't live on a cash basis. I must use credit cards.	I am managing my finances on a cash basis so I always know where I stand.
I can't live on my salary. It just isn't enough.	I am managing my money so I spend less than I make.
It's too hard to manage money.	I am a whiz at managing money.

I can never balance my checkbook.	Other people have learned to do this, and so can I.

Action Step 2: Develop a positive attitude about money.

Chapter 3
Debt Is a Four-Letter Word

He is rich who owes nothing.

~ Hungarian Proverb

Above all, if you are deeply in debt, pay cash for absolutely everything to prevent sliding any further into the hole. If you can't pay cash, you can't afford the purchase. Other than a mortgage, the one possible exception to this rule involves the purchase of a car. If you require a car, buy a pre-enjoyed car and pay off the loan as quickly as you can. If you have just finished school and carry a heavy amount of debt, buy the least expensive car available and enlist a roommate or two to share the rent on your home or apartment.

> **To get out of debt faster, start paying cash for everything.**

Pay off Credit Cards First

Resolving to pay cash, we still must tackle those pesky credit cards and credit card offers. No matter our financial status, credit card providers seem to barrage us with enticing invitations for new cards. The one simple reason: about 70 percent of credit card users carry a balance from month to month and, therefore, pay interest. That interest earns the credit card providers huge sums of money. Be aware that when you buy an item with a credit card and carry the cost of it from month to month, you generally end up paying at least 20% more for your purchase after the added interest. For example, that $100 meal really cost $120, and those $200 concert tickets actually took $240 out of your pocket with the additional interest that will be added over several years.

The credit card companies profit not only from the interest they charge. They also derive 30% of their profits from late fees as well as from penalty charges from customers who charge over the approved credit limit.

> **Credit card companies make more than 30% of their profits from penalties and late fees.**

One of the reasons that I have long believed that credit card companies throw so many credit card offers at college students is that they know many of them do not yet have good financial habits established. So even if a student only has a $200 balance on his or her credit card, the company can still make a quick $35 penalty fee if the individual is late on a payment or adds charges that exceed the approved line. Don't let this happen to you. Keep that money in your pocket rather than giving it to credit card companies for penalties.

Using a credit card is not only an expensive kind of debt, but it can also affect you in other unexpected ways. For example, the majority of young people turned down for mortgages find their applications rejected because of excess credit card debt. We'll cover this in more detail in a later chapter.

Many people don't keep track of what they charge during the month. When the credit card bill comes as a big, rude surprise, they realize they cannot pay off the charges. Don't let this happen to you. Remember, you want to be on the road to becoming rich, and having excess debt is a roadblock.

If you can't pay your credit card balances in full—at least 10 months out of 12, then grab a pair of scissors. Cut up all of your cards except for two to avoid this financial poison. Put one remaining card in your vehicle's glove compartment in case of a true roadside emergency. (If you can eat it, wear it, or drink it, this is not an emergency.) Put the other card in a desk drawer, or freeze it in a block of ice so it is not readily available while you shop. Once you quit using credit cards, you'll be amazed at everything you can easily go without.

If you can't pay your credit card balances in full each month— at least 10 months out of 12— then cut them up.

Note the exception if you own a business or if you travel for your employer and are reimbursed for your travel expenses: You might want to consider having a credit card to use exclusively for such business expenses. Using a credit card will make your record keeping much easier. Booking a hotel room or obtaining a rental car is also easier with a credit card. The same rules apply as above, however: You need to be sure to pay the card in full at least 10 months out of 12.

A caveat for college students and recent graduates: Don't be seduced by the deluge of credit card offers you will receive in the mail! A much better idea for many students is a debit card. It looks and functions just like a credit card, but the funds are deducted directly from your checking account immediately, rather than building up over a month and costing you interest if you don't pay off the balance.

Consider using a debit card rather than a credit card, particularly if you can't pay off your credit card in full every month.

Pay off Debt Quickly

Devising a strategy to put your existing debt behind you is easier than you think. The trick is to put your plan into writing, which will also get you out of debt much faster. Your mind is like a guided missile that needs to be programmed for a target. If you write down your target (or goal) of paying off all your debt on a certain schedule, your brain will go to work to make the goal a reality.

Here's a simple method: Divide a piece of paper into five columns or create a worksheet on your computer. In the first column, list all your debt: credit cards, car loans, furniture loans, loans for electronic equipment or major appliances, student loans, and any loans from your parents for a house down payment, etc. Next, list the balance of each account. In the third column, list the monthly payment for each obligation. In the fourth column, note the interest rate.

The chart below offers an example of what this might look like.

Debt	Balance	Monthly Payment	Interest Rate	
School loan	$12,000	$98	5.5%	
Credit card 1	$800	$38	9%	
Credit card 2	$2,200	$114	14%	
Credit card 3	$1,750	$96	18%	
Furniture loan	$725	$25	0%	
Car loan	$8,900	$250	7.5%	
Owe to doctor	$1,400	$40	18%	
TOTAL	$27,775	$661		

Before filling in the fifth column, you will formulate a method for paying off the debt sooner. For starters, if you are currently living hand-to-mouth, you *immediately* need to stop incurring unnecessary expenses that are deepening your financial hole. If this is the case, your big step forward will be figuring out how to generate more income. Is there a way to turn your favorite hobby into some extra cash? Is there a way to expand what you are already doing in order to increase your income? Do you own something you can sell on eBay?

Consider taking a second job for a while, putting 100% of your earnings toward paying off your debt. I am impressed with how many people wait tables as a side job in order to produce extra income. Many of them tell me they only work two nights a week but use those earnings to pay off debt or save for something extraordinary. How powerful would it feel to earn extra money every month and pay off your debt quickly!

Once you have mapped out your plan, revisit your debt repayment plan and fill in the empty fifth column with the newly increased monthly payment for each obligation.

Organize Your Plan, Dive into Action

Before we go any further, use a clean piece of paper or set up a new worksheet on your computer to list each item of debt in order. Put the obligation with the highest interest rate in the number one position and continue down the list, concluding with the item having the lowest interest rate. Using our example, let's say that you have increased your income or decreased your expenses to pay off an additional $300 of debt each month. This is now your priority list, as you'll be paying off the most expensive debt first:

Debt	Balance	Old Payment	Interest Rate	New Payment
Owe to doctor	$1,400	$40	18%	$340
Credit card 3	$1,750	$96	18%	$96
Credit card 2	$2,200	$114	14%	$114
Credit card 1	$800	$38	9%	$38
Car loan	$8,900	$250	7.5%	$250
School loan	$12,000	$98	5.5%	$98
Furniture loan	$725	$25	0%	$25
TOTAL	$27,775	$661		$961

Here's where the fun starts! Instead of paying your doctor $40 per month, you'll pay $340 and knock out the balance in five months. Once that is paid, add the $340 to the $96 you're

23

already paying each month for the third credit card. Paying $436 per month will have that card paid off within four months after the doctor's loan is paid. Now add the $436 you've been paying to the $114 you pay monthly for the second credit card, for a total of $550. If you keep going down the list, you will find yourself out of debt surprisingly quickly. Keeping up the $961 every month, you'll be out of debt in about three years, assuming you don't add any new debt while paying this off.

Each time one debt is paid off and crossed off your list, have a little celebration. When you pay off all the debt, reward yourself (remember to pay cash!) and quit that second job.

In the meantime, declare to your friends that you have a specific goal to become free of debt. When you turn down a $75 concert ticket that you cannot afford, you can smile and say, "Sorry, but buying a ticket conflicts with my goal of becoming totally free of debt. I'll go to a concert with you when I am free of debt and can pay cash for my ticket."

Cut Your Spending

When trying to spend less money, simply avoid stores whenever possible and watch less TV. Not spending money is amazingly easy when you don't have commercials and other temptations under your nose! Be aware: Big advertisers spend millions of dollars each year learning how to creep into your subconscious mind to make you feel as if you aren't living unless you own their products.

Think of simple ways to save money so you can spend less each month. Again, take in a roommate or rent a room rather than maintaining an entire apartment. Carpool or take public transportation to save gas and parking expenses. Pack bag lunches, at least part of the time, to save versus eating out. Hit the resale shops rather than the shopping malls. Invite friends over for popcorn and a rented movie. Walk your dog in the park while visiting with a friend.

Cutting your spending will allow you to see quicker results.

Credit Counseling

If you are really in a pickle and require more assistance to make headway, perhaps you'll want to consult with a credit-counseling firm. These organizations are listed in the phone book and online under "credit counselors." Be sure to pick a firm that is a nonprofit organization, as some of the for-profit firms have a reputation for taking advantage of people. One of my favorites is Consumer Credit Counseling Service (www.cccsinc.org). By using clear and specific goals, the professionals there can help you devise a plan for digging out from under all that debt.

An excellent resource for improving your financial situation on your own is http://www.ftc.gov/bcp/conline/pubs/credit/repair.htm. The service is provided through the Federal Trade Commission of the U.S. government.

If you need credit counseling, choose a nonprofit agency.

Another idea to consider is changing jobs to obtain better benefits, especially health insurance. If medical expenses are eating up a big part of your budget, working for a larger employer which offers more in benefits can be equivalent to a pay raise, even if your salary stays the same; the expenses you currently pay yourself would be paid by insurance. Many teachers have spouses who have become successful entrepreneurs. Why, then, do they continue to teach, other than that they love kids? The medical insurance is a compelling reason they both choose and remain in the profession, since medical insurance is so expensive for entrepreneurs.

Education Boosts Your Earning Power

Think about going back to school. If you want a long-term solution to paying off debt and having more money to save, nothing can beat education. I'm sure you have seen the charts that compare the median incomes for those with a high school diploma, some technical education, a college degree, a master's degree, and a professional degree, such as an MD or JD. Almost always, the higher the education, the higher the income people earn on average. (I temper this advice with the suggestion that you consider a state school rather than a private school if you are currently heavily in debt.)

Many receive a huge jump in salary with more training. One of my clients quit work for 18 months to acquire her MBA. Her income tripled within a few years of earning her advanced degree, and then doubled again within the next five years. Yes, she had to borrow money to pay for the education, but the loan was easy to pay off with her higher income.

Naturally, not everyone who returns to school will experience such a dramatic increase in income. If you work in a field that is not known for generous salaries, I'd urge you to get a cost-effective education at a community college or state school.

> **If you want a long-term solution to paying off debt and having more money to save, nothing can beat education.**

If you are considering going back to school to increase your earning power, put something in writing to motivate yourself. For example, when I was 27 and working fulltime at a bank, I decided to earn my MBA.

I took just one course per semester so that I could continue working fulltime while preserving enough free time to enjoy life. Because my undergraduate degree was in psychology, I had to take many prerequisites—eight classes in all—before I could even begin the MBA course. Because I'd be taking four classes a year, I knew in advance that I needed five years to complete this degree.

My brain was programmed like a guided missile! Making my goal a reality was such an intense desire that when I reached the fifth year and had just three classes remaining, I took a leave of absence from work to attend fulltime for the eight-week summer session to finish those last three classes in one fell swoop.

From the time I started my MBA in early 1977 until I finished the program in mid-1981, my income tripled. Was I three times as smart? Of course not! But going back to school and sticking with my plan sure told my boss that I was the kind of disciplined employee he wanted. Gaining more education is about acquiring so much more than what you learn. It shows your employer your ambition and work ethic. It says that you will work harder than the average person. If all things are equal except for education, you are more likely to be hired or promoted if you go the extra mile for more training.

Pay off Student Loans

More than 15 years ago, a friend who had borrowed close to $100,000 to finance her undergraduate and graduate degrees from a prestigious university landed an excellent job making a six-figure income. Despite that, she was paying only the minimum payments on her student loans. I urged her to accelerate the debt repayment to pay the loans off in just a few years rather than the 15 years allowed in the loan agreement. She questioned my sanity when I suggested something so radical, yet she did it!

Sometime later, she was working with a large company whose client was involved in a high profile scandal. That scandal took down her employer—and her job along with it. All of a sudden, she had quite a different perspective on that debt. She told me she was so glad that she had followed my advice. Although she had no job, she also had no debt and she had saved money once the debt was paid off. What she possessed was a financial cushion that allowed her the luxury of finding the job she truly wanted, all without the pressure of accepting a new job quickly in order to pay bills and keep up with debt payments.

If you have student loans, pay them off as quickly as possible.

You can always lose your money and your possessions, but you will never lose your education or the knowledge you've attained. As I mentioned previously, even if a millionaire goes broke, he or she typically sets out again to earn another million.

Remember: Debt and savings are polar opposites. You must save money if you want to become rich and it is much easier to do so if you are debt free.

Action Step 3: Get out of debt and stay out of debt.

Chapter 4

A Simple Guide to Becoming Financially Independent

Money is the seed of money, and the first dollar is sometimes more difficult to acquire than the second million.

~ Jean Jacques Rousseau

The Rule of 72

Why did Albert Einstein call the magic of compound interest the eighth wonder of the world? It came from a simple concept called the "rule of 72." Essentially, you divide 72 by the interest rate your money is earning, and that is how long it will take your money to double.

For example, assume you start with $4,000 when you are 22, and the money earns 10% a year, every year. Applying the rule of 72 (72 ÷ 10= 7.2), we find that your money will double in 7.2 years. The buildup would look like this:

Age	$ Amount
22.0	4,000
29.2	8,000
36.4	16,000
43.6	32,000
50.8	64,000
58.0	128,000
65.2	256,000
72.4	512,000
79.6	1,024,000
86.8	2,048,000
94.0	4,096,000

Isn't it staggering to know that $4,000 put away at age 22 will grow to about $4 million when you reach age 94! While growth during the first 40 years is impressive, the accumulation is truly mind-boggling during the last 30. (Note that the rule of 72 is a rough estimate. With annual compounding at 10%, you will actually have $3,822,375 at age 94. But that's not too shabby!)

Divide 72 by the interest rate your money is earning to approximate how long it will take your money to double.

Looking at this chart, we can easily understand why people who are born into wealthy families are nearly always bound to be wealthy! Can you imagine if money were put away regularly for you, beginning when you were a baby, and you didn't touch it for 60 years?

For this reason, I say repeatedly that getting rich is easy, especially if you are willing to become rich slowly—say in 30 or 40 years! Clearly, the phenomenal compounding begins to be quite powerful after 30 years. Unfortunately, the vast majority of people in the United States don't start saving until they are in their 30s or 40s…or even their 50s.

If you learn nothing other than the magical power of compound interest, this book will be worth its weight in gold to you. Can you see how *critical* it is to begin saving money as young as you possibly can? If you want to be extremely comfortable and financially independent someday, begin saving 10% of your gross income the moment you begin working, if you possibly can.

If you want to be financially independent someday, begin saving 10% of your gross income the moment you begin working.

What is financial independence? Simply put, it means having enough money invested so that you can live off the income from your investments without having to earn a cent from working. Does that capability mean that you'll quit working? Maybe not! Many wealthy, financially independent people keep working in their 50s, 60s, and 70s because they can afford to do the work they love without regard to how much money they need to earn.

Plan to Save 30 Years

Saving enough to be financially independent generally takes 30 years. When you hear about people who are financially independent in their 50s, more than likely they started saving when they were in their 20s. Those who start in their 30s are usually financially independent in their 60s. And those who don't save until their 40s or later (or never!) are the ones who must continue working in their 70s and 80s.

Once you have saved money for your financial independence, don't touch it! Don't use it for a house. Don't touch it to send the kids to college or to live on when you change jobs. Pretend it is in a magical trust fund that you aren't allowed to touch until you retire.

Company-Sponsored Savings Plans

A 401(k) plan, if you have one at work, usually provides the best means to save for your financial independence. Your company will typically match part or all of what you save. If you work for a nonprofit organization, such as a school, church, hospital, charity, etc., you will probably have access to a 403(b). A 401(k) and 403(b) are quite similar, with the main distinction being whether your employer is a company or a nonprofit.

> **A 401(k) or 403(b) plan at work will usually provide the best means to save for your financial independence.**

If you are either self-employed or work for a small company, a SEP IRA or a SIMPLE IRA might be available to you. You should be aware that the majority of small employers offer no retirement plan at all. An IRA is an Individual Retirement Account. A SEP or SIMPLE IRA is a type of IRA that can be offered through a small business.

If your company offers "matching," leap at the opportunity to take advantage! Typically, the company will match 3-6% of the amount of salary you contribute to your retirement account. Matching, then, can equate to as much as an incredible 100% return on your investment. If you invest $2,000 and the company matches dollar for dollar, you immediately have $4,000 invested, which is a 100% return—all because you are an employee. You can't find that kind of return anywhere, so don't pass it up!

> **If your company offers matching, take advantage of it!**

What's the catch? Most often, companies follow a vesting schedule. This means the percentage of the company match which you are eligible to keep depends on the number of years you work for the employer. A common vesting schedule is 20% per year for five years. In other words, you can keep 20% of the match if you leave the company after one year of service, 40% if you leave after two years, 60% after three years, 80% after four years, and the full 100% after five years.

On top of the matching from your employer, the other huge benefit of a 401(k) plan is the ability to deduct the total amount that you contribute to your retirement from your taxable income, both federal income taxes and state income taxes. Let's say your income is $60,000, which falls within a 25% federal tax bracket and a 6% state tax bracket in our example. If you save $6,000 in your 401(k) plan, you will reduce your federal taxes by 25% x $6,000—or $1,500, plus 6% x $6,000—or $360 in state income taxes. Ultimately, saving $6,000 for retirement is partially funded by $1,860—or $1,500 + $360—in tax savings; as a result, your reduction in take-home pay was only $4,140—not $6,000!

I have to stress again that your goal is to save 10% of your income for at least 30 years. Therefore, when you save 7% of your earnings and your company matches with 3%, if you are vested, you will be meeting your goal. An additional bonus is that you will not pay federal, state or local taxes on this money that you save from your paycheck. (You will, however, pay social security taxes.)

Roth IRAs

A Roth IRA is your best alternative if: your company does not offer a retirement plan; the plan offered has little or no matching provision; or you would like to save more than your company plan allows. You will pay income taxes before the money is invested, but once the after-tax money is in your account, that amount will grow tax-free *for the rest of your life!* In my experience, this is easily the best tax benefit the government has ever allowed. Again, an IRA is an Individual Retirement Account, and a Roth IRA is named after Senator Roth who sponsored the legislation to create this type of IRA.

> **The Roth IRA is the best tax-advantaged savings the government allows. Use a Roth (if you are eligible) after you take advantage of company matching in a company plan.**

Again, you're probably wondering what the catch is. The only stipulation is that you can have a Roth IRA only if your adjusted gross income is less than $95,000 per year if you are single, and it must be less than $150,000 per year, combined with your spouse's income, if you are married. (You can do a partial contribution if you are slightly over these numbers.)

Roth IRAs present another wonderful benefit: They are not subject to the required minimum distribution rules that apply to all other IRAs and qualified retirement plans. In other words, when you succeed in saving for a comfortable retirement, you will never have to take a required withdrawal on your Roth. Traditional IRAs mandate taxable payments to you every year starting after you are 70 ½ years old.

We'll go into more detail about IRAs and 401(k) plans later in the book, when we discuss investing your money and opening your first retirement account.

I have included some compound interest rate charts to impress upon you the importance of saving early to allow your money time to grow. Carefully review the charts so that the numbers sink in. Only 18 of 100 people will earn an annual income that is greater than $30,000 per year at retirement. (Source: Social Security Administration, Office of Research and Statistics, April 2000.) The other 82% will fail to plan. Decide that you will be among the 18%, and start saving immediately!

The first chart assumes that you start saving at the age of 22 and stop at age 40. The example also says that you save $300 per month—or $3,600 per year—as soon as you graduate, and that you increase the amount you save by 3.5% a year to keep up with inflation. Another assumption says that you are earning a conservative 7% on your investments.

After age 40, you might concentrate on your children's school expenses, and, therefore, never manage to save another dime for financial independence. Not to worry! You will already have saved a total of $94,886. And since you won't touch the money until you are 65, over the years this will grow to over $1 million, which will help fund your independence! Wow! Less than $95,000 will grow to $1 million!

Get Your Assets in Gear!

	Start saving immediately, stop at age 40			Start saving at age 32, stop at 65	
<u>Age</u>	<u>Savings</u>	Balance	<u>Age</u>	<u>Savings</u>	Balance
22	3,600	3,852	22	0	0
23	3,726	8,108	23	0	0
24	3,856	12,802	24	0	0
25	3,991	17,969	25	0	0
26	4,131	23,647	26	0	0
27	4,276	29,878	27	0	0
28	4,425	36,704	28	0	0
29	4,580	44,174	29	0	0
30	4,741	52,339	30	0	0
31	4,906	61,253	31	0	0
32	5,078	70,974	32	3,600	3,852
33	5,256	81,566	33	3,726	8,108
34	5,440	93,096	34	3,856	12,802
35	5,630	105,637	35	3,991	17,969
36	5,827	119,267	36	4,131	23,647
37	6,031	134,069	37	4,276	29,878
38	6,242	150,133	38	4,425	36,704
39	6,461	167,556	39	4,580	44,174
40	6,687	186,440	40	4,741	52,339
41	0	199,490	41	4,906	61,253
42	0	213,455	42	5,078	70,974
43	0	228,397	43	5,256	81,566
44	0	244,384	44	5,440	93,096
46	0	279,796	46	5,827	119,267
47	0	299,381	47	6,031	134,069
48	0	320,338	48	6,242	150,133
49	0	342,762	49	6,461	167,556
50	0	366,755	50	6,687	186,440
51	0	392,428	51	6,921	206,896
52	0	419,898	52	7,163	229,043
53	0	449,291	53	7,414	253,009
54	0	480,741	54	7,673	278,931
55	0	514,393	55	7,942	306,954

Start saving immediately, stop at age 40			Start saving at age 32, stop at 65		
Age	Savings	Balance	Age	Savings	Balance
56	0	550,400	56	8,220	337,236
57	0	588,929	57	8,508	369,945
58	0	630,154	58	8,805	405,263
59	0	674,264	59	9,114	443,384
60	0	721,463	60	9,433	484,513
61	0	771,965	61	9,763	528,875
62	0	826,003	62	10,104	576,708
63	0	883,823	63	10,458	628,268
64	0	945,690	64	10,824	683,829
65	0	1,011,889	65	11,203	743,684
Total	94,886	1,011,889	Total	228,431	743,684
Difference	133,545	268,205			

If you save a total of $94,886 by age 40, and you don't touch any of the savings until you are 65, at 7% interest, you will have over $1 million to help fund your independence!

The columns on the right assume you don't start saving until you are 32. If you save the same $300 per month, increasing the amount by 3.5% each year, you will have saved $228,431 by the time you are 65. Even though you will have saved approximately $228,000 (or $133,000 more than the previous example), you will have amassed only $743,684 (or $268,000 less than if you had started saving when you were 22) by the time you reach age 65.

Isn't it amazing that saving a mere $200 each month when you are 22 is much more powerful than saving $400 per month when you are 32?

My mom taught me that saving money is a decision and a habit. That philosophy has helped me tremendously. Never assume that saving will be easier when you make more money. The theory simply is not true! If you only knew how many people I have met who earn well over $100,000 per year yet have never saved any money to speak of. Think of the movie and sports celebrities who earned millions per year in their 20s but ended up homeless or on welfare by the time they reached their 40s or 50s. The number of zeros in one's income does not matter if the individual fails to save.

Decide right now that you will save a percentage of your income, no matter what. You will be so glad one day when you are financially independent!

Saving money is a decision and a habit, not a function of your income.

If 10% is too big a bite from your income right now, start with something. If your money situation is extremely tight, you should at least save 1% or 2%. Having acquired the habit of saving is more important than the actual amount you have accumulated. Just start somewhere, increasing the percentage later when you earn more. If you see that you can put away only 1%, consider taking in a roommate or finding other ways to cut expenses to create more available funds to save.

The following chart assumes you will start saving immediately upon graduating college and stop at 65. Clearly, starting in your 20s makes a huge difference. The left column shows that one who begins at age 22 saves only $42,233 more than does the person who begins 10 years later. However, because savings began at such an early age, the compounded difference in the money at age 65 is $611,185. *Wow!*

Like many of the older people who attend my seminars, you may be close to tears right now if you are 35 or 40 or older. You may be moaning to yourself, "Why didn't I learn this when I was 22?" If this is you, give copies of this book to the younger people in your life! You can see what a big favor you would be doing for them. Also, begin using this information to your best advantage now.

Start saving immediately, stop at age 65			Don't save until age 32, continue until 65		
Age	Savings	Balance	Age	Savings	Balance
22	3,600	3,852	22	0	0
23	3,726	8,108	23	0	0
24	3,856	12,802	24	0	0
25	3,991	17,969	25	0	0
26	4,131	23,647	26	0	0
27	4,276	29,878	27	0	0
28	4,425	36,704	28	0	0
29	4,580	44,174	29	0	0
30	4,741	52,339	30	0	0
31	4,906	61,253	31	0	0
32	5,078	70,974	32	5,078	5,434
33	5,256	81,566	33	5,256	11,438
34	5,440	93,096	34	5,440	18,059
35	5,630	105,637	35	5,630	25,348
36	5,827	119,267	36	5,827	33,357
37	6,031	134,069	37	6,031	42,146
38	6,242	150,133	38	6,242	51,775
39	6,461	167,556	39	6,461	62,312
40	6,687	186,440	40	6,687	73,829
41	6,921	206,896	41	6,921	86,403
42	7,163	229,043	42	7,163	100,116
43	7,414	253,009	43	7,414	115,057
44	7,673	278,931	44	7,673	131,321
45	7,942	306,954	45	7,942	149,012
46	8,220	337,236	46	8,220	168,238
47	8,508	369,945	47	8,508	189,118
48	8,805	405,263	48	8,805	211,778
49	9,114	443,384	49	9,114	236,354
50	9,433	484,513	50	9,433	262,992
51	9,763	528,875	51	9,763	291,847
52	10,104	576,708	52	10,104	323,088
53	10,458	628,268	53	10,458	356,895
54	10,824	683,829	54	10,824	393,459
55	11,203	743,684	55	11,203	432,988

Start saving immediately, stop at age 65			Don't save until age 32, continue until 65		
Age	Savings	Balance	Age	Savings	Balance
56	11,595	808,149	56	11,595	475,704
57	12,001	877,560	57	12,001	521,845
58	12,421	952,280	58	12,421	571,664
59	12,856	1,032,695	59	12,856	625,436
60	13,306	1,119,220	60	13,306	683,454
61	13,771	1,212,301	61	13,771	746,031
62	14,253	1,312,413	62	14,253	813,504
63	14,752	1,420,067	63	14,752	886,234
64	15,269	1,535,809	64	15,269	964,608
65	15,803	1,660,225	65	15,803	1,049,040
Total	364,458	1,660,225	Total	322,225	1,049,040
Difference	42,233	611,185			

You'll want to note that my examples applied 7% as the hypothetical interest rate. The S&P 500 stock index long-term average has ranged between 10% and 11%, while bonds and certificates of deposit typically average between 4% and 9%. Therefore, my assumed 7% rate fits a middle-of-the-road investor who has both stocks and more conservative investments in his or her portfolio.

Unbelievably, a few of my clients have actually gone overboard in saving. By living extremely frugally in their youth, they had accumulated $5 million or more when they reached their 60s. I have urged several of my clients in their 40s and 50s to save less and enjoy today more. If you are saving 10% of your income for the future, and you are sure you will never need to touch your cushion until retirement, do enjoy spending now!

If you are a huge saver, be sure to include funds for vacations, hobbies, entertainment, and other pleasures in your financial plan. You will enjoy life so much more if you maintain a balance between saving for the future and enjoying the present. I was raised so frugally that spending money for the pleasures in life was once an issue for me. Now I've found a balance between saving and enjoying today. I can rest assured that the 10% I've saved for over 30 years guarantees the financial independence that I want.

Maintain a balance between saving for the future and enjoying the present.

If you are over 50 years old and broke, then there's a good chance you've spent too much money having fun the previous 30 years; therefore, it's time for you to buckle down and save at least 15-20% each year! The last thing in the world you want is to be financially dependent on your children, all the while perpetuating a cycle of dependency. How can they save for their own independence if your kids are supporting you?

If you are older and just starting to save money, your kids might object that you are not as generous with them as you used to be. If that's the case, explain to them that you have become serious about preparing for your financial independence. Help them understand that they should be grateful because they won't have to support you one day. When my Mom told me that when I was 16, I wasn't exactly impressed (I just wanted some new shoes, darn it!), but I grew to be appreciative later, in my 30s, 40s, and 50s with the awareness that I would not have to support her.

If you are an older person who has not saved enough for independence, invest in your health. It is the best and quickest way to stretch your budget. Get as healthy as possible. While you can't change the fact that you haven't yet saved much money, you definitely can influence your health, starting this minute. Begin with exercise. Reduce your blood pressure and cholesterol levels. Lose weight. Don't be a candidate for diabetes, cancer, or heart disease—all of which have been linked to being overweight and out of shape. Tell yourself that this healthful lifestyle can possibly help save you $500 each month in medical bills, especially as you get older.

> **If you are older and have not yet saved much for your
> financial independence, the best investment you can make
> right now is to get as healthy as possible.**

My sister Kim, now in her fifties, is as thin as most people in their 20s. I was telling her one day how proud I am of her for staying so trim, and she told me, "Oh, Jan, you know the main reason I do it is because I'm too cheap to give my money to doctors!" She has a good point.

How Long Will It Take to Be a Millionaire?

The one point I want you to grasp is this: No matter what you earn, if you save 10% of it, you will be rich someday. Exactly when that day will be does depend on your income, but it *will* happen. The following charts provide some powerful examples.

These are examples showing an income of $25,000 a year, then $50,000 a year, then $100,000 per year. In each one, we assume you save 10% of your income and this increases 3% a year as you receive pay raises. For simplicity in the math, we'll say you invested all money on the last day of the year. Our assumed earnings rate on the money is 8%.

How long will it take to be a millionaire?

Year	Salary	Save	Earnings	Balance
1	25,000	2,500	0	2,500
2	25,750	2,575	200	5,275
3	26,523	2,652	422	8,349
4	27,318	2,732	668	11,749
5	28,138	2,814	940	15,503
6	28,982	2,898	1,240	19,641
7	29,851	2,985	1,571	24,198
8	30,747	3,075	1,936	29,208
9	31,669	3,167	2,337	34,712
10	32,619	3,262	2,777	40,750
11	33,598	3,360	3,260	47,370
12	34,606	3,461	3,790	54,620
13	35,644	3,564	4,370	62,555
14	36,713	3,671	5,004	71,230
15	37,815	3,781	5,698	80,710
16	38,949	3,895	6,457	91,062
17	40,118	4,012	7,285	102,359
18	41,321	4,132	8,189	114,679
19	42,561	4,256	9,174	128,110
20	43,838	4,384	10,249	142,742
21	45,153	4,515	11,419	158,677
22	46,507	4,651	12,694	176,022
23	47,903	4,790	14,082	194,894
24	49,340	4,934	15,592	215,419
25	50,820	5,082	17,234	237,735
26	52,344	5,234	19,019	261,988
27	53,915	5,391	20,959	288,339
28	55,532	5,553	23,067	316,959
29	57,198	5,720	25,357	348,035
30	58,914	5,891	27,843	381,770
31	60,682	6,068	30,542	418,379

Year	Salary	Save	Earnings	Balance
32	62,502	6,250	33,470	458,100
33	64,377	6,438	36,648	501,186
34	66,308	6,631	40,095	547,911
35	68,298	6,830	43,833	598,574
36	70,347	7,035	47,886	653,495
37	72,457	7,246	52,280	713,020
38	74,631	7,463	57,042	777,525
39	76,870	7,687	62,202	847,414
40	79,176	7,918	67,793	923,124
41	81,551	8,155	73,850	1,005,129

How long will it take to be a millionaire?

Year	Salary	Save	Earnings	Balance
1	50,000	5,000	0	5,000
2	51,500	5,150	400	10,550
3	53,045	5,305	844	16,699
4	54,636	5,464	1,336	23,498
5	56,275	5,628	1,880	31,005
6	57,964	5,796	2,480	39,282
7	59,703	5,970	3,143	48,395
8	61,494	6,149	3,872	58,416
9	63,339	6,334	4,673	69,423
10	65,239	6,524	5,554	81,501
11	67,196	6,720	6,520	94,741
12	69,212	6,921	7,579	109,241
13	71,288	7,129	8,739	125,109
14	73,427	7,343	10,009	142,460
15	75,629	7,563	11,397	161,420
16	77,898	7,790	12,914	182,124
17	80,235	8,024	14,570	204,717
18	82,642	8,264	16,377	229,359
19	85,122	8,512	18,349	256,220
20	87,675	8,768	20,498	285,485
21	90,306	9,031	22,839	317,354
22	93,015	9,301	25,388	352,044
23	95,805	9,581	28,163	389,788
24	98,679	9,868	31,183	430,839
25	101,640	10,164	34,467	475,470
26	104,689	10,469	38,038	523,976
27	107,830	10,783	41,918	576,677
28	111,064	11,106	46,134	633,918
29	114,396	11,440	50,713	696,071
30	117,828	11,783	55,686	763,539
31	121,363	12,136	61,083	836,759

Year	Salary	Save	Earnings	Balance
32	125,004	12,500	66,941	916,200
33	128,754	12,875	73,296	1,002,371
34	132,617	13,262	80,190	1,095,823
35	136,595	13,660	87,666	1,197,148
36	140,693	14,069	95,772	1,306,989
37	144,914	14,491	104,559	1,426,040
38	149,261	14,926	114,083	1,555,049
39	153,739	15,374	124,404	1,694,827
40	158,351	15,835	135,586	1,846,248
41	163,102	16,310	147,700	2,010,258

How long will it take to be a millionaire?

Year	Salary	Save	Earnings	Balance
1	100,000	10,000	0	10,000
2	103,000	10,300	800	21,100
3	106,090	10,609	1,688	33,397
4	109,273	10,927	2,672	46,996
5	112,551	11,255	3,760	62,011
6	115,927	11,593	4,961	78,564
7	119,405	11,941	6,285	96,790
8	122,987	12,299	7,743	116,832
9	126,677	12,668	9,347	138,846
10	130,477	13,048	11,108	163,002
11	134,392	13,439	13,040	189,481
12	138,423	13,842	15,158	218,482
13	142,576	14,258	17,479	250,218
14	146,853	14,685	20,017	284,921
15	151,259	15,126	22,794	322,840
16	155,797	15,580	25,827	364,247
17	160,471	16,047	29,140	409,434
18	165,285	16,528	32,755	458,717
19	170,243	17,024	36,697	512,439
20	175,351	17,535	40,995	570,969
21	180,611	18,061	45,678	634,708
22	186,029	18,603	50,777	704,087
23	191,610	19,161	56,327	779,575
24	197,359	19,736	62,366	861,677
25	203,279	20,328	68,934	950,939
26	209,378	20,938	76,075	1,047,952
27	215,659	21,566	83,836	1,153,354
28	222,129	22,213	92,268	1,267,836
29	228,793	22,879	101,427	1,392,142
30	235,657	23,566	111,371	1,527,079
31	242,726	24,273	122,166	1,673,518

Year	Salary	Save	Earnings	Balance
32	250,008	25,001	133,881	1,832,400
33	257,508	25,751	146,592	2,004,743
34	265,234	26,523	160,379	2,191,646
35	273,191	27,319	175,332	2,394,296
36	281,386	28,139	191,544	2,613,979
37	289,828	28,983	209,118	2,852,080
38	298,523	29,852	228,166	3,110,098
39	307,478	30,748	248,808	3,389,654
40	316,703	31,670	271,172	3,692,497
41	326,204	32,620	295,400	4,020,517

Did you let the numbers sink in?

Below are the summarized results:

If you earn $25,000 a year, you will have $1 million in 41 years.

If you earn $50,000 a year, you will have $1 million in 33 years. In 41 years, you will have $2 million.

If you earn $100,000 a year, you will have $1 million in 26 years. In 41 years, you will have $4 million.

Now it should be clear why I say that most will need to save 10% of their earnings for 30 to 40 years to build a comfortable retirement.

If it hasn't jumped out at you, let me offer another point: Even if you double your income from $25,000 to $50,000, at the same time doubling your savings, you will accumulate your first $1 million only 8 years sooner. Isn't that fact astonishing? The charts should plainly show you the power of compound interest. Saving when you are young—allowing your savings 30 or 40 years to compound—is what *really* makes you rich!

Another point is equally compelling: If you look at the example of earning $50,000, you'll notice that it takes 26 years to save the first $500,000. However, in year 33, just 7 years later, the second $500,000 has been accumulated. Then in year 38, just 5 years later, the third $500,000 has been added. A mere 3 more years is needed to add the next $500,000. Of course, you are not only adding new savings to the account, but you are earning an investment return on all the money that is already saved.

> **In our example, it takes 26 years to save the first $500,000, 7 years to save the second $500,000, 5 years to save the third $500,000, and just 3 years to save the fourth $500,000.**

If you are reading this now as a 20-something-year-old, yeah! By all means, find the motivation to start saving right now. And if you've passed your 20s, don't despair. Start saving right this minute and catch up.

How Much Is Enough?

If you are younger, use the rule of thumb of saving 10% of your gross income. If you are of an age at which you are seriously considering retiring, you will want to do a more specific calculation. And it's actually easier than you think. Start by writing out a spending plan that considers how much money you think you'll need each year. Don't be surprised if this number is the same as what you are spending now or even more!

Once you feel comfortable with the number, subtract the amount that will be provided by pensions, annuities, or social security. Next, take what's left and multiply it by 25. That total will give you an estimate of how much you will need in savings to retire, keeping up with inflation, for the remainder of your lifetime. Therefore, if you think you need $40,000 a year more than your pension and social security to live comfortably, you will need to accumulate 40,000 x 25 = $1,000,000. If your calculations indicate that you will need $75,000 more per year than pensions and social security, you will need 75,000 x 25 = $1,875,000.

How did I pick 25 as the number to multiply? It is based on the assumption that you will earn about 7% per year on average on your investments. It assumes that you will live on 4% of the earnings and reinvest the other 3% in order to keep up with inflation. Consequently, if you have $1,000,000 and you earn 7%, you would live on 4% or $40,000 and add the other $30,000 you earned to your investment account. The next year you would have $1,030,000 x 7% or $72,100. You would live on 4% or

$41,200 and reinvest the other $30,900. So each year you will be able to take out a bit more from your investment account in order to keep up with inflation.

Of course, if you do follow such a strategy, you will never diminish the amount of your investment account since it grows each year. If you want to use a bit of the investment principal each year—and so cause your remaining balance to equal $0— then perhaps you could multiply by 20 rather than 25 to determine the size of the investment pool you will need. The only hitch with multiplying by 20 is the eventuality that you live to 102 and run out of money. Generally, the safe number to use for your calculation is 25.

Action Step 4: Save 10% of your gross income for financial independence.

Chapter 5

Do You Hate Budgets?

A budget is telling your money where to go instead of wondering where it went.

~ C. E. Hoover

Does it surprise you that the typical millionaire writes out a formal spending plan and then consistently tracks his or her spending? It shouldn't, as living by a written spending plan and saving enough to become a millionaire are highly correlated.

> **Most self-made millionaires use written spending plans to track their spending.**

As we have plainly stated, getting rich is simple. The two most critical actions to making it happen are staying out of debt and saving money on a consistent basis. If you carry debt and you don't save money, you're probably thinking, *that doesn't seem simple to me!* Therefore, simply put, you need a formal spending plan!

A Spending Plan Is a Roadmap to Lead You *Away* From Debt and *Toward* Saving Money

As with any other journey, the way to riches requires a map so that you can reach your pot of gold quickly without unnecessary detours. You probably wouldn't drive from Boston to San Francisco without a good roadmap, so why make your journey to financial wellbeing without a plan?

Unfortunately, most people start spending money without a thought. First, they do not take time to figure out where they currently stand. Second, they cannot imagine where they are going. No wonder they end up taking endless detours! Until you know how much money you have coming in and going out each month, you will not have control over your financial destiny. You cannot control what you cannot measure!

To begin any journey, you clearly have to know where you are at the start. So where are you? Do you know exactly how much debt you carry? Do you know exactly how much you must spend each month for your fixed expenses, such as rent, utilities, and loan payments? Do you know how much of a margin you have between how much you earn and how much you must pay each month?

Only the rarest person makes financial progress without a written spending plan. It lets you see in advance how your money is allocated, making it easier to remain on course by saying no to the budget busters.

A spending plan is also rewarding because it lets you spend without guilt. For example, let's say you are free of debt and saving money every month. You decide that taking a vacation to Italy is important, and you plan to spend $3,000 for the trip. You can then begin to save $300 every month. Once the day arrives, you will enjoy spending every cent because you will have both the peace of mind and satisfaction of knowing that you earned and saved the cash for that very purpose. You can take your trip without guilt because you are on track with your savings goals, and you are not incurring debt.

A spending plan lets you spend without guilt.

Self-Made Millionaires Are Frugal

People who don't possess much money usually don't know the secret shared by most self-made millionaires: They are extremely frugal! I hope that one day you will read a book called *The Millionaire Next Door*. The authors, Thomas Stanley and William Danko, conducted interesting research showing that only about 20% of the millionaires in this country inherited their wealth. The other 80% earned it themselves! (Yes, we've touched on this before, but it certainly bears repeating.)

Their research shows that typical self-made millionaires buy used cars. They rarely buy expensive homes or lavish furniture. They typically live in the same home for 20 years or more. They shop at garage sales and resale shops. They also buy discounted items at Marshalls or T.J. Maxx, not high-ticket clothing from Nordstrom or Lord & Taylor. How's that for being frugal?

I fall in that self-made millionaire category. When I was married in 1992, I wanted good dress clothes for my boys to wear at the wedding. However, since the church we attend is casual, I knew it was unlikely that the boys would ever wear the fancy clothes again. I decided to shop at Goodwill for the items they needed. Does that surprise you? The idea came from several friends of mine who had been doing that for years, and none of them are poor.

I also buy most of my evening gowns at secondhand shops. I love $800 party dresses, but I don't want to pay much more than $100 for a dress. In all the times I have received compliments on a dress, never once has anyone asked the price or where I bought it!

> **Consider shopping at secondhand shops for expensive items that are not used frequently, such as party clothes, to stretch your spending plan.**

Notice that I have never used the word *budget* here. But clever person that you are, you probably realize that a spending plan is another word for budget. Why change the name? Most people regard a budget in the same way they feel about diets: *Yuck! If I can't have this and I can't have that, I'm going to be miserable! I work hard for my money—and I want to enjoy it!*

Let me urge you to consider a major attitude shift about saving and spending. If you can't gain a positive perspective, then you are unlikely to make the effort. Or you'll "try" only for a short period of time before abandoning the idea. Look at your spending plan as your way to choose a specific strategy to become rich someday. Realize that you're copying the habits of most self-made millionaires. Recognize it as ensuring that you will have the money you need to buy what really matters to you, rather than wasting dollars on things that don't mean anything.

> **Look at your spending plan as your way of setting specific goals in order to become rich someday.**

For example, my two big loves are clothes and travel. I want to be sure that I have money every year for these two pleasures. They are at the top of my discretionary spending list. I don't care as much about restaurants and driving fancy cars. So when we go out to dinner, we are much more likely to choose restaurants where the total tab for my husband and me will be $20 or $40 as opposed to $75 or $150. Combined with all the money I save driving used cars, I can splurge on clothes and travel. I'm telling my money where to go—to suit me!

Write Out Your Spending Plan

So how do you create a spending plan? It's easier than you think.
- Write down the total income you will receive after taxes.
- Pay yourself first (savings):
  - 10% for financial freedom
  - Savings for a house
  - Savings for a car
- Find a way to help others in need by giving some away.
- Figure out how much is left and decide how to live on it.

A spending plan has two phases, the first of which is setting up the plan. This entails writing down what you intend to spend. The second phase is tracking what you actually spend. It doesn't do a bit of good to write out a spending plan and never track your actual spending. If you write down that you'll spend $100 per month on clothes, for instance, but never know how much you actually spent, what good is that?

Now, let's set up a spending plan. If you have never tracked your spending before, consider using a simple index card system—my mother taught me that trick. Once you get the hang of it, you may want to begin using Quicken, Money, or another financial software. However, if you are one of the many who find such software overwhelming, just use a simple method that works.

To start, pretend the table on the following page is an index card. You will prepare a card like this for each month of the year. To simplify, we will assume taxes have already been withheld from the paycheck.

Sample Index Card System

Net income (after taxes)	2,200	
Expenses:		
Rent	600	
Electricity	50	
Cell phone	55	
Car loan	180	I recommend saving this for your next car once the loan is paid off.
Insurance	70	
Charity	100	
Credit card	175	
401(k)	200	
Gas-car	90	
Groceries	175	Write down the amount each time you visit the grocery store. Example: 26 38 15 51 19 22 = 171
*Lunches out	135	
*Entertainment	100	
*Travel	100	
*Clothes	100	
*Miscellaneous	100	
Total	2,230	

*Put most of these in cash envelopes. (We'll discuss this in a moment.)

Let's suppose this is your spending plan. Notice that the spending of $2,230 is more than the income of $2,200, and that no money is allocated for repairs, medical expenses, emergencies, saving, or anything else unexpected. If you knew in advance that every penny of your take-home pay was committed, you'd realize how important it was to say *no* to a $200 unplanned shopping trip. It would also tell you that you couldn't spend a total of $2,230 every month for the various categories. You have to figure out where to cut back on your expenses.

Resolve to stay out of debt, save 10% for your financial independence, and live on the rest without overspending on credit cards.

You will also note that nothing is budgeted for expenses that might occur quarterly or once each year, such as car tags, Christmas/holiday presents, club membership dues, pest control, or other miscellaneous expenses. As you begin to track your spending, you will become more aware of these "budget busters." A good way to handle them is to add up the total for the year, then divide by 12. Put the calculated amount into savings each month. When such expenses pop up, simply withdraw the money that you've put aside in savings to pay for them.

Now that you have the expenditures written out, think about how you can change some of the numbers so that your spending is more in line with what you truly want in life. For instance, if you are like many people I know, having only $100 each month for entertainment and only $135 a month for lunches out would be way too little! Meanwhile, other areas of spending could be less.

For instance, if you decided $600 a month is too much for rent, you might opt to find a roommate to share your apartment. A roommate would cut your current rent in half to $300 a month. Another option is to find a larger apartment for $800 a month, and sharing this larger one with a roommate decreases your monthly portion to $400.

You may decide that $100 a month, or $1,200 a year, is not nearly enough for travel since that is your greatest passion. You might increase this area to $150 a month and cut your clothing expenses to $50 a month. (Perhaps the idea of shopping at Goodwill now makes sense to you, too!)

Track Your Actual Expenditures

Remember to use a new index card each month, saving each one so you can total the figures at the end of the year. As the month progresses, you will also use the spending card to track your actual spending.

I like to put all of my recurring expenses at the top of the list. Then, when I pay each bill, I simply put a checkmark next to the amount. In other words, if I wrote a check to the landlord for my rent, I'd put a checkmark next to the $600.

For the variable expenses, such as groceries, record the actual money you spend each time you go shopping next to the budgeted amount. For example, if my grocery budget is $175 a month, that line might look like the one in the sample chart.

What if you overspent, making the total $215? You'd have two choices. You could determine that you are going to stick to $175 each month, which means you have to start grocery shopping more frugally. Or you could decide that $175 cannot be stretched to buy the groceries you want. If you end up with a higher grocery budget, you will need to decide what other category you are going to cut so that the outflow does not exceed the inflow.

If your outflow exceeds your inflow, your upkeep will be your downfall!

When I used the index card system, I kept the card on me at all times. Every time I spent money, I jotted down the amount on the appropriate line on the index card.

Write out what you intend to spend each month, and then jot down what you actually spent in each category.

Many people develop written spending plans and then find they can't stick to them. When they track their spending, they notice that they go through several hundred dollars at the ATM without ever knowing where the money went. If you find yourself in a similar situation, consider using a simple "envelope system." After you determine how much to spend on meals out, entertainment, gifts, sports and hobbies, etc., put money aside for each of these categories into separate, individually labeled envelopes. The money in the envelopes is yours to spend for the entire month. When the cash is gone, stop spending!

On that note, we come to the number one reason that credit cards are such a budget buster. We decide to spend $100 a month on entertainment, for example, but if a tempting situation arises, we give in by charging it. In doing so, we don't pay attention to the fact that we've now spent more than the amount we earned for the month.

Especially to avoid the habit of building credit card debt, I recommend that you use a spending card to track *all* of your spending, whether with checks, debit card, credit card charges, or ATM cash withdrawals. (For simplicity, I would enter the ATM withdrawal as a single amount rather than itemizing each purchase.)

What if Nothing Is Left?

Becoming aware of the fact that what you spend in one area impacts another is one of the major benefits of a spending plan. When you overspend in one area, you must find a way to cut another.

I am always awed by people who do not save any money at all each month, and yet they will spend $4 at a fancy coffee shop without giving it a thought. By spending $4 a day for 30 days, a person spends a total of $120 per month, or $1,440 per year. To determine the long-term impact of this example, we'll make the calculation extremely simple by ignoring inflation completely. If a person continues the habit for 30 years, while you, the very wise person, decide to save $4 per day, you will have accumulated $196,282 if we assume an annual interest rate of 9 percent. Think about it: Three decades from now, would you rather say that you had a cup of gourmet coffee every day, or would you rather have $196,000 in investments?

Now, I'm not saying *never* to splurge or treat yourself to various delights. I am only advising to be conscious about your choices and to make deliberate decisions. Know that the spending decisions you make today will make a big difference in your financial situation 30 years from now.

> **The spending decisions you make today will make a big difference in your financial situation 30 years from now.**

Pay Yourself First

I highly recommend that you adhere to the old adage: *Pay yourself first*. In truth, your taxes will be paid first, but the next 10% should then be put into long term savings. Afterwards, live on what is left over. You'll notice in our example that you are saving $200 a month in your 401(k) plan at work, which is less than 10% of your gross income. Where could you reduce your spending in order to save a full 10%?

Over the years, I have observed many who save automatically every month in their 401(k), but they don't use spending plans; consequently, they run up credit card debt every month for the spending that exceeds their take-home pay. If they are laid off, become ill, or are unable to work for any reason, they typically end up spending the money in the 401(k) plan for everyday living expenses.

For this reason, I say repeatedly that if you want to be rich one day, you must stay free of debt *and* save money regularly. If you save money but accumulate debt, at some point you will end up using the savings to pay off the debt. In the end, you will never get ahead.

As I was writing this book, I e-mailed numerous friends, asking them what they most wished someone had told them when they were young. Without a doubt, the most common response was wishing someone had taught them how important it is to start saving money early in order to take advantage of years of compound interest. Incidentally, when questioned, both my clients and those who have attended my seminars overwhelmingly gave the same response. Many said that they were never able to save any money because they never had a spending plan. Thus, they spent every penny they earned, and more!

> **When asking older friends what they wished they had learned about money in their 20s, overwhelmingly they regretted not being told how important it is to start saving as young as possible.**

One of my favorite stories came from a friend who loved having her nails manicured every week for $25. Her wealthy uncle told her she should switch to every other week. If she saved $25 x 26, ignoring inflation, she would have $650 after one year. If the money earned 9% per year, she'd have about $99,000 after 30 years, $253,000 after 40 years, and $632,000 after 50 years. Wow!

Yes, $25 sounds like a nominal amount to most people, but seeing how much the amount can compound over time gives a completely different perspective.

Why have I spent so much time on this topic? Few people successfully remain free of debt *and* save money unless they have a written plan. There are a few exceptions, I'll admit, but they truly are exceptions. All of my financial planning clients are affluent. One factor most have in common is that they track their spending every month and they pay themselves first.

> **Few people can remain free of debt *and* save money without a written plan.**

If you are 35 or younger, an extra reason should motivate you to remain free of debt and save. Your grandparents, and probably your parents, will have their retirement years supplemented by Social Security. However, the possibility exists that Social Security will be bankrupt by the time you want to retire. Economists have been beating the drum with Congress for years to do something to avert such a train wreck, but so far nothing meaningful has happened.

Simply put, if you don't save for yourself, you may be sunk. Most people I know who are still working when they reach their

70s and 80s are in one of two categories: The first category includes those who are financially independent but choose to work at something they truly love to do; the idea of being home all day is boring to them.

The second category is the one you don't want to be in. These people have to work because they can't afford groceries and medicine otherwise. They often become financially dependent on their children. Sadly, their dependency perpetuates the cycle, as the children spend their money supporting the parents rather than saving.

What if you create your spending plan only to discover that you must spend every penny you earn in order to live? If this is your finding, don't be discouraged. The situation is quite typical. And the two common solutions are obvious: Earn more money or spend less. If you know of a third way to tackle this, please let me know!

Earlier we mentioned earning more income, especially to get out of debt. Consider a second job. If you are a stay-at-home parent, research home-based businesses that would allow you to earn income while still caring for your children.

For some people, earning more money is not possible. In many cases, the income itself is not the root of the issue. Believe me—many families with incomes of $100,000 a year and more don't save a dime! Saving money is about making a decision and a commitment; in fact, saving is more a function of mindset than income. If you don't save a dime when you earn $50,000 a year, you probably won't when earning $100,000 or $150,000.

Saving is not so much a function of your income level. People earning $100,000 a year often have just as much trouble saving as those who earn $40,000 a year.

In December of 2005, Yahoo! Finance published a survey of how much it costs to live an upper-middle-class life in America. Their definition of the demographic included having two quality cars, private schools for the kids, a second home, and a fine, four-bedroom, 4,000-square-foot home. Supporting such a lifestyle required an income of $200,000 to $500,000, depending on where one lived. The most interesting statistic in this study was that the families who made such an income showed an *average* savings rate of 1% of their income! So please never delude yourself into thinking that when you earn more money, you will automatically save more money.

If you can't earn more, the obvious next step is to evaluate your spending to decide where you can cut back. Car expenses are a good area to assess. Upon realizing that the monthly payment plus the insurance, gas, and maintenance total as much as 20% of their overall spending, many people who take my seminars decide they must sell their expensive cars. Others determine that they are in over their heads with a house that costs far too much, and they downsize or even rent for a few years while making a concerted effort to get out of debt.

If you are saving nothing now, I urge you to develop a plan to make it happen. And start now! In the beginning, you should aim to put away at least 3% of your gross income. Each time you earn a raise, save as much of that money as possible so that you can increase the percentage until it reaches 10%.

I can't say it enough: The ultimate goal, indeed the magic number, is to save 10% of your gross income for 30-40 years in order to become financially independent. Because this 10% is for your eventual financial independence, it is not to be touched. For more immediate wants, start a second savings fund.

> **Pay yourself first by ensuring that the first 10% of your income goes to your savings for financial independence.**

Set Specific Goals

We discussed goal setting earlier, but clarifying objectives is especially relevant to creating a spending plan, as well as in carrying out any other component of finances. Never underestimate the power of setting goals!

When I was married in my 20s, my then-husband and I agreed that we would always pay cash for everything, except the mortgage on the house. When we were first married, we saved just over 10% of our incomes. Each time we earned a raise, we would save about 60% of the increase, with the rest going to taxes and usually something fun like a vacation. After we were married several years, we bought a house with considerable property, which was ideal for our shared passion for tennis. Within a year, we had saved the money to have a tennis court installed. A year or two later, we put in a swimming pool, again with cash. We later added a big deck to the back of the house.

We lived in that house for nearly 10 years before we had furniture in every room. Some of our friends would laugh at us. They thought it was too funny that someone could afford a tennis court and a swimming pool, but not furniture. We would smile and say that we were committed to paying cash for everything, and we'd decided the "toys" were much more important than furniture, especially since we were young and hadn't yet had children. I was asked more than once if I wasn't embarrassed to invite people over to a home without furniture. Isn't that thinking typical of those who believe they must keep up with the Joneses?

Is it your goal to keep up with the Joneses, or do you have other priorities?

If you have ever taken a self-improvement seminar or read any self-improvement books, you know that they all stress the importance of goals. To be considered a goal rather than a wish or a dream, it must be written, it must be clear and specific, it must be measurable, and it must have a time limit. If you have never written out goals, start now. You will be astonished by their power, which is almost supernatural. As you review your goals frequently, your mind sends up special antennae that seek opportunities that allow you to achieve them. Think about it: The mind controls your actions the way a military commander controls a missile. Your brain requires a solid target—a goal—the same way a missile must be programmed to hit a specific target.

When my husband and I married in 1992, he had tons of debt and no spending plan. Moreover, although he was nearly 51, he had only a few thousand dollars in his 401(k) plan. As you might guess, I was scared to death about marrying him and later ending up in a real financial mess. I told him not to marry me unless he would agree to a written spending plan, a commitment to pay off his debt as soon as possible, a commitment to save for our financial independence, plus a commitment to tithe 10% of our income to charity. Otherwise, I knew we would fight endlessly about money.

Being the clever guy that he is, he agreed. Based on our income, expenses, and debt, I wrote out a spending plan, which indicated we would require five years to pay off the debt. With persistence and frugal living, we were debt free—with the exception of the mortgage—in just over two years. I can't tell you how many friends and clients have told me similar stories of success when they set goals. Other than debt, what have *you* got to lose by setting a target to hit?

Never underestimate the power of setting goals.

Stretch Your Spending Plan

Let's now look at some other ways to stretch your spending plan. If you aren't currently saving at least 10% of your income, consider limiting yourself to no more than one expensive hobby. When I was in my 20s and 30s, many of my friends were skiers and often invited me to join them. I decided that although skiing would be a blast, I could not afford all the equipment and travel expenses while also funding my favorite sport, which was tennis. I wanted the money for new tennis equipment every year, as well as an annual week at a tennis camp. I simply could not maintain both hobbies and still have enough money left to meet my savings goal.

Buying extravagant gifts is another way that many people blow their budgets. Imagine if you wrote out your complete spending plan and realized that you could only afford $50 a month, or $600 per year, for gifts. Many people spend much more than that in December alone. With the addition of birthday, wedding, and baby gifts, you would be deep in the hole!

Decide in advance how much is reasonable for your spending plan and stick to it! Consider personalized homemade gifts, which can cost considerably less than purchased gifts, especially for wedding and baby presents. Convey to your family and close friends that you don't want to hurt anyone's feelings, but you are choosing to reduce your gift expenditures so you can stay on track with your spending plan.

I personally had to take such action when I was a divorced single mom of two little boys. So they would not take personal offense at the absence of gifts the first Christmas after my divorce, I contacted all my friends and family members to tell them I was buying only for the children (nieces and nephews) and pleasantly requested that they do the same for us. I received an overwhelmingly positive response, with many friends confiding what a relief it was to cut down on the gift buying. To this day, I keep the list short and sweet, and I certainly enjoy December far more as a result.

Can you stretch your spending plan by cutting back on expensive hobbies or gifts?

At the same time, I was training my children to give meaningful, personal gifts rather than expensive presents that often go unused or unappreciated. My boys both know the way to warm my heart is to give me pictures and a card with a meaningful handwritten note. Moreover, I appreciate flowers more when I receive them unexpectedly. They can be far less expensive at a time other than Valentine's Day.

What if you have a written spending plan, but "retail therapy" is your thing? If it's a big problem for you, you may want to consider counseling or a 12-step group. Don't laugh! Many who spend far more than they can afford are inadvertently compensating for an issue or pain they don't want to face. Without facing the problem, the overspending probably won't go away.

For others, a strategy of staying away from the stores, the TV shopping channels, or internet shopping sites is sufficient. At the very least, decide on a spending limit when you go shopping. There's nothing wrong with wanting to buy something to make yourself feel better when you feel blue, so if your spending plan allows you to purchase $75 on clothes this month, then go ahead without guilt!

Some people use charge cards to record their spending because each monthly bill itemizes and categorizes everything. This method works so long as you pay attention to your totals. If you overspend one month, be sure to compensate by spending less the following month. For instance, if your monthly budget for clothes is $150 yet you spend $225 on an outfit one month, be sure to allow only $75 for your clothing budget the following month.

And keep in mind that those who shop with cash tend to spend about 20% less than do people who use credit cards. Amazingly, you will consistently spend less if you have to use cold, hard cash! When I say cash, I mean greenbacks, debit cards, and checks. Test yourself for a month or two and you will see how true this is!

> **People who shop with cash rather than credit generally spend about 20% less.**

Give Your Mental Attitude a Checkup

Remember when we talked about attitude? Nowhere is your frame of mind more important than in being capable of living in line with your spending plan. If you tell yourself it's too hard or you can't do it, sure enough, you won't. Therefore, choose a more empowering thought. Tell yourself that if other people can do this, you have the power as well. Tell yourself that you are determined to achieve your goals, and you now hold the ticket to reach your ultimate destination in life. Remind yourself that the best way to be successful is to imitate what successful people do. Self-made millionaires use spending plans, so decide it is smart to imitate them. Make up your mind and make it happen!

How Much In Each Category?

Frequently, people ask me how much money they should allocate to each area of spending. Age typically determines the answer more than any other factor. If you're younger, you will likely spend more on items like appliances and furniture. If you're older, you'll typically spend more on medical expenses and repairs.

For instance, let's assume your age ranges between 21 and 30, and you live in an apartment. You're still single, but you dream of marrying in the next few years. The idea of being financially independent when you are in your 50s or 60s sounds terrific, so you want to save for that period of life. You want to be a self-made millionaire, and you realize that living frugally is the right path. You also believe in giving some away to those less fortunate and to causes that are important to you. Your monthly spending plan might look like this chart.

Gross income (before taxes)	100%	2,750
Expenses:		
Taxes	20%	550
401(k)	5%	140
Charity	5%	140
Rent	20%	550
Electricity/gas – home	4%	110
Cell phone	2%	55
Car loan	7%	195
Gas – car	3%	80
Insurance	5%	140
Debt/credit card	8%	220
Travel/entertainment/gifts	6%	160
Clothes/haircuts/miscellaneous	6%	160
Food/lunches out	9%	250
Total	100%	2750

Many would consider an annual income of $33,000 to be decent for someone in his or her 20s, yet the reality of seeing how a person of such means would be pushed to the limit—even with spending numbers that aren't extravagant—is sobering. Therefore, I offer the following general rules of thumb:

- Spend 25% or less of your gross income on housing (rent or mortgage), utilities, upkeep, house taxes, lawn care, etc.
- Spend 10% or less of your income on car expenses, including your loan payment, gas, maintenance, etc.
- Spend 10% or less of your income on food and dining out.
- Save 10% or more for your financial freedom. If you can hardly live on your current income, how will you manage when you are 75 and you must spend $300 each month for medicine?

Spend 25% or less of your gross income on housing, 10% or less on car expenses, 10% or less on food, and 10% or more for your financial freedom.

Again, Stay out of Debt!

In our example, a big chunk (8%) goes out every month on the credit card and debt payment. Wouldn't becoming free of debt—and staying out of debt—be more appealing? If so, you could raise your savings from 5% to 10% and have another 3% for travel, entertainment, clothes, or other pleasures.

What if you already carry heavy credit card debt or major student loans, and much more than 8% of your income is needed for repayment? As we discussed earlier, taking on a second job and using 100% of your extra take-home pay to lower your debt could be your most practical solution. Additionally, take the next smart action of no longer using credit cards at all. Under no circumstances do you want to dig the hole any deeper!

Now let's assume you are 32 and married. You have bought a house, and your first baby is on the way. Your combined income of $80,000 sounds like a good amount, but you never seem to stretch the money quite far enough. Here's how you might prepare your spending plan for the first year after the baby is born:

Gross income (before taxes)	100%	6,667
Expenses:		
Taxes	20%	1,330
401(k)	5%	335
Charity	5%	335
Mortgage/house tax	20%	1,330
Electricity/gas/upkeep – home	5%	335
Childcare	12%	800
Baby expenses/doctors	3%	200
529 college savings	3%	200
Cell phones	2%	135
Car loan (or savings)	5%	335
Gas – car	3%	200
Insurance	4%	265
Travel/entertainment/gifts	3%	200
Clothes/haircuts/miscellaneous	3%	200
Food/lunches out	7%	467
Total	100%	6,667

Notice that *nothing* is budgeted here for debt, furniture, or appliances. Meanwhile, some of the other numbers are probably far lower than what people in this income bracket actually spend. Does this change your perspective on writing out a spending plan when you see all the categories laid out like this? The major benefit my spending plan presents to me is the awareness that the amount out cannot be more than the amount in. Clearly, if I want to splurge in one area, I have to decide in which area(s) I will cut back.

Prepare for Emergencies

Set up a savings account in which you will save one month's living expenses within 18 months of when you start working if you possibly can. Increase the savings account to two months' living expenses within three years, then to three months' expenses after that. This particular account will be your official emergency fund that will be used only if an illness or a layoff temporarily prevents you from earning a paycheck.

> **Set up a savings account that will eventually contain three months of living expenses for your emergency fund.**

Always decide in advance how you will allocate your money, and then track your actual spending to see how well you are aligned with your goals and financial decisions. Treat your spending plan as a game, and determine to emerge victorious. Also, be aware that, as with any game, you won't know the score if you don't keep score—or in this case, keep track of where your money goes.

For more guidance, I recommend a resource that contains excellent information about starting a spending plan: http://www.personalfinancebudgeting.com/.

Action Step 5: Use a spending plan to track your money, to get out of debt, and to begin saving.

Chapter 6

Better to Own Your Car Than for Your Car to Own You

We are the first nation in the history of the world to go to the poorhouse in an automobile.

~ Will Rogers

Shouldn't it go without saying that it is critically important to consult your spending plan before you shop for a car? Of course, you want to know exactly how much of a car payment you can handle before you fall in love with a vehicle you cannot afford. What, then, is your guideline? You don't want to spend more than 10% of your gross income for the car payment, gas, maintenance, and insurance. Also, even if you earn a huge income and find yourself in a strong financial position, I would recommend that you never borrow more than $20,000 for a car. If you can afford that Mercedes, Lexus or BMW, then pay all cash or at least a partial cash down payment.

| **Keep your car expenses to 10% or less of your income.** |

Drive Previously Enjoyed Cars

Self-made millionaires typically drive used cars. Moreover, they usually buy rather than lease. If it's good enough for millionaires, isn't it good enough for you? I am amazed to see how many kids immediately buy expensive new cars upon graduation. After talking with many of them, I realized how seriously young people view their cars in terms of status. Many believe that the type of car one drives represents success or failure. If you drive a cheap-looking car, your friends and everyone else in the world will think you must have a crummy job, right?

If you think about the situation for a minute, you'll realize that we covered this topic in Chapter Two. Your beliefs about money will drive your spending habits and likewise influence the type of car you drive. Fortunately for me, my parents repeatedly said how foolish it was to waste money on new cars. With that in mind, when I saw a friend with a pricey car, I'd think he or she was foolish, not successful.

When I'm driving along the interstate and see an expensive car, I assume the vehicle is leased. I further presume that the driver is broke because she spends all her money trying to keep up with the Joneses. All of my clients have $200,000 or more invested with me. I've had only one couple leave my practice because they fell below my minimum. Guess what type of cars they drove? A Jaguar and a Corvette!

One of my clients, in her early 40s, is an extremely diligent saver. Until recently, she drove a 10-year old Honda. If she keeps saving the way she does (about 20% of her income), she will be financially independent when she is 50 years old. Her dream is to be a full-time artist. Would you rather drive a fancy car or be able to live your dream when you are 50?

On a side note, although I love spending frugally and therefore buy used cars, I won't tolerate a vehicle that looks cheap or shabby. Keeping your older car looking new is not difficult. Waxing the car frequently, at least twice a year, makes a huge impact. Maintaining a spotlessly clean vehicle also makes a significant difference. Amazing how much newer a car looks and feels when it is clean and shiny!

From 1998 until 2005, I drove two used Hondas. The first one was 10 years old when I sold it, and the second one was 12 years old. Neither car required any costly repairs; my expenditures included tires, batteries, and starters. Over this entire seven years of car ownership, I bought the two cars and sold them for a total outlay of $4,000. (I sold the first car for $2,500 less than I paid for it, and the second one for just $1,500 less.) Imagine how much money I saved during that time, especially since I didn't have much money going to car expenses.

On the other hand, my husband, who is crazy about cars, is much more willing to spend money on them than I am. Two cars ago, he spent $29,000 on a vehicle, drove it for six years, and then sold it for $9,000. Consequently, his net cost over six years was $20,000. When you're 70, would you rather have the money invested, or would you rather be able to say you drove a $29,000 car?

Always Buy, Never Lease

Never lease cars except in unusual circumstances. Always buy. Why? Over a 20-year period, people who lease spend far more on their cars than do those who buy. If you lease, you essentially trade in your car every two-to-three years, so you always pay for the front-end depreciation. People who buy their cars typically own them longer, so over time the average cost is less.

Buy your car rather than leasing!

Another secret: Don't trade in your cars often, especially if you are buying new cars. Many of my wealthy clients own their cars for five-to-seven years—and sometimes even longer. One of my delightful, very well-off clients drives a Mercedes. The car is 15 years old and has been paid in full for many years!

Pay Cash for Your Cars

The best way to keep your spending in check is to pay cash when you buy a car. I mean cold, hard cash—not cash borrowed from the bank. My mother taught me this trick as well, and I am especially grateful to her advice. She said that I should have goals that would enable me to pay 100% cash for my cars by the time I turned 40.

If you're a 22-year-old, you may think I've lost my mind! I understand that you're not likely to pay cash for such an expensive item. Therefore, I'll recommend some realistic guidelines for you to follow:

1st car – pay 20% cash; pay loan off in 4 years or less
2nd car – pay 40% cash; pay loan off in 3.5 years or less
3rd car – pay 55% cash; pay loan off in 3 years or less
4th car – pay 70% cash; pay loan off in 2 years or less
5th car and all future cars – pay cash!

Save in advance so you can pay cash for your cars.

If you are one of the lucky young men and women who received a car as a graduation gift or if you already own a paid-for car, then consider saving for your next car now. By the time you are ready to buy it, you will be able to pay cash. Why do I stress this point? Forking over $10,000 or $15,000 or $25,000 or $35,000 in cash is a heck of a lot harder than signing loan or lease papers that show only your monthly payment, whether it's $200 or $400 or $700 a month.

I liked my mom's advice so much that I began saving for my second car when I was 25. Since that time, I've paid cash for all but one. Believe me—if an unexpected financial challenge hits, you'll be happy you don't have a car payment. For instance, in 2005, my husband was unemployed for many months. How delighted do you think we were that we had no car payments—in fact, no debt other than a small mortgage?

Remember, in addition to the car payment, you must pay for gas, maintenance/repairs, annual license/tax fees, insurance, and any customizing expenses on your car. When you are considering how much to pay for your next car, be sure to factor all of these items into your spending plan.

When my son Brett graduated from Penn State in 2004, his father gave him money to buy a car. Brett shopped for many weeks to find the perfect deal. He ended up with a beautiful Honda with less than 40,000 miles, leather seats, and all the bells and whistles for $13,000. Many of his friends owned $25,000 cars, and my son marveled that his car looked every bit as sharp as theirs, yet his cost about half as much.

Within two months of obtaining his first full-time permanent job after college, he had started a savings fund for his next car. He is already committed to the idea of paying cash for every car he buys for the rest of his life. Brett wants to be financially independent before he is 40, and he knows that being frugal with car expenses is one of the ways he will be able to save for his financial freedom.

Car Buying Tips

When you are ready to shop for your next car, following a few tips will help you secure a better bargain. If you are buying from a dealer, always shop at the end of the month. Salespeople, who have monthly quotas, are willing to negotiate with you if they are in danger of not meeting their sales minimums. The smartest route is to shop for your next car between Christmas and New Year's to take advantage of both month-end and year-end quotas. We bought our last car on December 29, and even as magnificent bargain hunters, we were astonished with the fabulous deal we received.

> **Shop for a car at the end of the month, when the salesperson is trying to meet his or her sales quota.**

Often, buying a used car from the previous owner, rather than through a dealer, produces the best deal. I have bought four of my last five cars in this way, and I have been delighted with the results. Some states, like Georgia, don't require sales taxes when you buy from a private owner. For me, that alone delivers a 7% savings.

If you are willing to be patient, you can take advantage of the fact that others are sometimes desperate to get rid of their cars. For example, I paid $5,000 less for my last car than the previous owner still owed on her lease. After being hospitalized, she greatly needed cash. Two cars before that, I bought a sports car from a new father whose wife wanted to free up garage space for the new minivan. After having the car on the market for five months, he finally received an offer from me. No one else had bothered to respond to his ad because his asking price had been ridiculously high. He initially turned down my low offer. However, at his wife's insistence, he called me back two days later to accept!

If you simply must buy a new car, consider buying between October and December. Buy the previous year's model, which will probably be offered on closeout once new models are in the showroom. Remember, you are in a great bargaining position when taking the "obsolete" model off their hands.

You might wonder about purchasing a car with 0% financing from the dealer. Usually such an offer applies only to new cars, not used. Now, you already know I think you should pass on the new car; however, if you have your heart set on a new car and the dealer offers 0% financing *and* you have negotiated a good price for the car, the deal clearly makes good sense. If you have the cash saved up for the car, should you still use the 0% financing? I'd say *yes*, but make certain to keep the savings set aside. That way, if an emergency arises, you will be able to apply the cash for the monthly payments.

Again, never lease a car unless you want to be "car poor" your entire life.

Changing your beliefs is simple. The critical point is to *decide* that you will be the millionaire next door one day, while your friends in their new cars drive away their savings. *Decide* that having money tucked away is more important than trying to impress other people with your fancy car. Reward yourself in other ways. If your passion is travel, your money saved from not making car payments may allow you to crisscross the globe. And in addition to indulging your real pleasures, you'll also have saved for your financial independence.

Action Step 6: Buy previously owned cars rather than new cars. Develop a plan so that you have the capability to pay cash for your cars.

Chapter 7

Staying out of the Poorhouse when Buying a House

Cashtration (n.): The act of buying a house, which renders the subject financially impotent for an indefinite period.

~ *Washington Post* Style Invitational

Buying Your Home Makes Good Financial Sense

A central component of the American Dream is to own a house. Is it a smart financial move as well? Yes—most of the time! Home ownership makes sense if reasonable limits are placed on how much you spend for your house. Many people make the mistake of stretching too far to buy their first home, and then they become so cash poor that they can't afford to buy a pair of socks!

Again, I recommend that not more than 25% of your gross (before tax) income go toward housing expenses, which are comprised of everything you must pay to live in your home, including the following:

- Mortgage principal and interest
- Private mortgage insurance (PMI)
- Property taxes
- Property insurance
- Repairs and maintenance
- Utilities – gas, electric, water, sewer, garbage, alarm system
- Landscaping and yard upkeep
- Furnishings, window treatments, carpeting, flooring

Allocate no more than 25% of your gross income to housing expenses.

When we earlier devised a spending plan, remember how hard it was to find 10% to save? Think how hard it would be if your housing expenses were 30-40% of your income! And yet this is the situation so many people create. Don't let it happen to you. Just as you do when buying a car, be careful to write out your spending plan, knowing exactly how much you can allocate to housing expenses.

Many young people are barely able to make ends meet while living in apartments and paying $800 to $900 per month for rent and utilities. Then they buy homes with housing expenses of $1,500 to $2,000 per month, unfortunately learning firsthand the definition of "cashtration!"

People sometimes argue that the best approach is to stretch to buy the biggest house they can possibly afford, as a home is the best investment they will ever make. They plan to use pay raises to "grow into" their housing expenses. I completely disagree with such reasoning. Most people's homes aren't true investments. The popular trend is to move every five to ten years, each time buying a house that is not only more expensive, but also requires an even larger mortgage. While you will always need a place to live, you will need to eat as well. You cannot eat your house, nor can you buy clothes with it. You can't finance a vacation with your house either. Your house is the place you live, not an investment.

For a house to be a legitimate investment, you must eventually sell it, take the equity (the value of the home minus the mortgage debt), and invest that equity money into some sort of investment that you can live on. My experience as a long-time financial planner is that homeowners rarely operate in this manner. A financially comfortable person will generally buy a retirement house that is nearly as expensive as the home he or she was living in while working. In fact, oftentimes the retirement home will cost more!

Those who sell their houses and move to far less-expensive homes to live on the equity generally do so because they are broke; they desperately need the money for everyday living. Why are they broke? The likely answer has much to do with the overly expensive houses they purchased over the years. Ironically, attempting to pay for homes they couldn't afford prevented them from saving.

Wouldn't it be smarter simply to buy a more budget-friendly house from the beginning? That way, you know in advance (by writing out your spending plan) that you'll always be able to save at least 10% of your income for your future financial independence!

Buy a less-expensive house so you can save 10% of your income every year.

One notable exception is worth mentioning. People who live in California and New York City often pay double, triple, or even quadruple the housing expenses of other parts of the country. They often can sell at retirement and move to a state where the cost of living is lower, using their home equity for investments. If you reside in an incredibly expensive housing market, then the guidelines are much different for you.

Did you know that most millionaires live in the same house for 20 or more years, and that their housing expense as a percentage of their income is much lower than it is for the population as a whole?

Don't you think that is one of the reasons they become millionaires in the first place? When you are tempted to spend too much on a house, tell yourself that you intend to be a millionaire one day, and you know that millionaires are frugal with their housing expenses!

No-Money-Down Mortgages

The craze of buying a house with no money down is downright crazy! If you purchased a home with no down payment, you probably haven't saved any money to make a down payment. If that's the case, you likely don't have the financial discipline to own a house in the first place. I recommend that you save a minimum of 10% of the cost of your first home before buying. The savings ensure that you have the financial discipline required to keep up the mortgage payments and house ownership expenses.

Your home ownership expense is generally going to be more expensive than renting. Therefore, while you are renting, you need to be saving the difference between rent and housing costs. For example, if rent and utilities are $900 a month and the expected home ownership expenses are $1,600 a month, you need to start saving $700 each month. Using this example, let's say you plan to buy a $170,000 house. Putting aside $700 per month, you will take around two years to accumulate a 10% down payment.

Once you buy the house, you will have established the habit of paying $1,600 per month ($900 rent/utilities plus $700 savings), so handling your $1,600 per month of housing expenses should be easy. If you were paying $900 to rent and weren't able to save money, how would you be able to afford $1,600?

Sometimes people have to sell their home sooner than anticipated. What happens if you lose your job? What if you become too sick to work? What if you have a baby and can't work for a while? If you didn't put any money down and the home showed only a nominal amount of appreciation (increase in market value), you could actually lose money when selling the house.

On the other hand, if you had saved first and put down 10%, the likelihood that you could sell the house and come out ahead would be greater. If you were forced to sell the house because something bad occurred, wouldn't you want to walk away with some money in your pocket rather than losing your house *and* owing more money than your final selling price?

> **Plan to save first and then put 10% down when buying your first home.**

Remember, too, that most people buying their first houses also need to buy furniture, window treatments, new carpets, appliances, and myriad other things. If you haven't been able to save any money for the down payment on your house, how will you ever put aside money for your home's necessities? If you buy items on credit, the spending plan would require that you add those payments to the 25% housing expense that we previously discussed. Better still, in addition to saving for the down payment, put even more cash away for all such important extras.

Avoid PMI if You Can

Another major reason to save at least a 10% down payment is to avoid having to obtain private mortgage insurance, or PMI. Lenders typically require that you pay this insurance payment to the bank or mortgage company if you do not make a 20% down payment when buying your house. Obviously, PMI increases your cost of home ownership. If you buy a house with 0% down, you can be sure you will have to pay PMI.

However, if you make a 10% down payment, many lenders will offer "piggyback financing" for another 10%. Thus, your first mortgage will be only 80% of the cost of the house, and you will not need to pay for PMI. The piggyback financing is a second mortgage on the house, and it will be paid as a separate loan. If you obtain piggyback financing on your house, challenge yourself to a game of paying it off in record time!

If for some reason you are the exception and actually have a good reason to buy a house with no money down, you probably already know that such loans are available.

Consider Buying a Fixer-Upper

Purchasing a fixer-upper makes sense for first-time homebuyers. Have you heard the term *sweat equity*? Again, equity is the value of a possession, minus the debt on it. If you have a home worth $150,000 and your mortgage is $135,000, then your equity is $15,000. If, for instance, you perform repairs and improvements that cost you $10,000 but allow you to sell the house for $180,000, then you have created $20,000 of sweat equity (the increase in the value of your home after deducting the $10,000 cost of improvements).

I have met many young couples who followed this advice. They bought ugly first houses in good neighborhoods. Then they painted, replaced fixtures, updated the kitchens, gussied up the bathrooms, added wallpaper, and lived in the house for a few years. It's not unusual to walk away with $50,000-$100,000 worth of sweat equity upon selling the home three-to-five years later. The additional equity they earn creates a substantial down payment for the second home. Not only can they buy a better home, but putting so much money down keeps the new mortgage affordable.

Nevertheless, do beware. Some fixer-uppers become endless money pits. Be sure to do your homework carefully so you face only cosmetic issues, not major structural damage.

> **Consider a fixer-upper for your first home to build sweat equity.**

Stores like Home Depot and Lowes can become your best friends. In addition to selling the products you'll need, such home improvement stores offer contractor services and installation services for major projects. Compare their prices versus the estimates private contractors provide for the same job. You may find considerable savings.

Save Money on Your Mortgage

Let's say you are about to buy your first house. You have the perfect home in mind, and the payments are within your spending plan. Two crucial steps allow you to save money on your mortgage expense. The first is to buy a credit report with your FICO score. If you have a score of 700, that's great. If it's 760 or higher, congratulations! You'll probably qualify for the lowest interest rate loan available. If your score is close to the critical number, pay down your credit cards as much as possible to improve your score before applying for a loan. The effort will save you a ton of money over the long-term by qualifying you for a lower interest rate.

The second step is to *shop around* for a good mortgage rate and low points. Most real estate agents will have a favorite mortgage broker and will recommend you to that person. Sometimes you will obtain a good deal, but don't count on it. Why? Most real estate agents will refer you to the mortgage broker who refers business to them: You scratch my back, and I'll scratch yours!

Use the Internet to shop rates. In less than an hour you'll gain a strong feel of what a good rate is. Next, search for specific companies' websites. My recommendation is to find one with a local office. If you're in Boston, for example, you don't want to do business with a mortgage company in Denver just because of a good rate on the Internet. My advice comes from personal experience.

About eight years ago, I shopped for a mortgage on the Internet. The only thing good about my experience was the interest rate. Everything else was a nightmare, and closing on the mortgage took well over 60 days. We experienced delays even though my husband and I had perfect credit along with 50% equity in the home. They obviously had no hassle whatsoever confirming our good credit!

Alternatively, we bought a new home three years ago. I shopped for the loan on the Internet, but then worked with a local contact of the bank that I chose. What a difference! The local broker was a dream to work with, and we had everything closed in less than 30 days.

The mortgage company makes money in two primary ways: on the interest rate and on the "points" you pay. Points are nothing more than an expense to you in order to provide extra profit to the lender. One point is equal to 1% of the mortgage amount. Sometimes you will acquire what seems like a low interest rate only to learn that you are paying many points. Beware! This is one way lenders take advantage of young borrowers. Obviously, you want the lowest interest rate and the lowest points you can possibly obtain, especially if you think you will live in your house for only a short while or if you plan to refinance the mortgage after a short time. If you anticipate being in the house quite a long time, paying more in points in order to reduce your interest rate can make sense.

Shop around for a good mortgage interest rate, low points, and low closing costs, but work with someone local.

Another critical item to consider when you buy a house is a home inspection. Hiring a quality home inspector ensures a professional will look over the house and provide a reliable list to you of all the necessary repairs. Once you have this list, you may be able to negotiate with the seller to cover the costs. In some cases, you may decide you don't want to own the home at all, especially if the inspector finds structural damage or termite damage.

Fixed-Rate or Adjustable-Rate Mortgage

Your interest rate can be either fixed or adjustable. As implied, a fixed rate means that you pay the same interest rate every year. If you plan to be in the house for many years, a fixed rate is usually the right choice. Generally, fixed-rate mortgages will cost more than adjustable-rate mortgages in the first years. However, paying a bit more upfront for the assurance that the interest rate will never increase is worthwhile.

If you acquire an adjustable-rate loan, you will pay a certain interest rate for a certain period, and then the rate will "adjust" to the current interest rate level. Each loan is different, so you need to read the fine print. Will it adjust in one year, in three, or in five years? Then, after the first adjustment, how many years pass before future adjustments will be made? Does a limit or cap exist on how much the rate can change?

If you think you will be in a home for a short period, then an adjustable-rate loan will often make more sense. For instance, if you are a corporate gypsy who moves every three-to-five years, you will want to jump on the opportunity to obtain a five-year adjustable rate loan, meaning your interest rate is locked in for the first five years. We acquired a five-year adjustable rate loan when purchasing our current house because we intended to pay the mortgage in full over that five-year period; therefore, what the rate adjusted to later would not matter to us. Conversely, when purchasing our previous home, we were likely to live there at least 10 years, until our children graduated, so we obtained a fixed-rate loan.

If you think you will live in a home for a short period, then an adjustable-rate loan will often make sense.

In addition to a fixed versus an adjustable rate, you will also be able to choose between a 30-year, 20-year, or 15-year mortgage. Other repayment periods are available, but the three mentioned are the most common.

If you are young, I recommend obtaining the 30-year loan if the payment would only narrowly keep you on track with your spending plan. On the other hand, no matter your age, if your high income can handle the payments for a 15-year loan while you maintain the 25% of income guideline for your housing expenses, then leap on the opportunity for a shorter mortgage. You'll be surprised how quickly 15 years will pass!

Also, make sure that your mortgage comes with no prepayment penalties; otherwise, you'll have to pay a penalty if you choose to prepay any of the principal before it's due. Let's say you buy a house with a 30-year mortgage, and your housing expenses are 25% of your income when you first buy the house. Several years later, your good pay raises and bonuses give you a substantial cushion of extra cash. You might choose to begin paying extra amounts on your mortgage every month in order to pay it off in 15 or 20 years instead of 30. Wouldn't it be fabulous to own your house free and clear? (Many people set a goal of paying off their mortgage before their children go to college so extra money is available each month to help cover school expenses.)

If you are 50 or older, you surely want to secure a 15-year mortgage. You'll want to have your house paid in full by the time you retire to ensure you financial independence. If you claim that this isn't reasonable because your payments would be too large, my advice is to consider buying a less-expensive house! If you can't own it free and clear by age 65 or 70, the home is outside your price range.

> **Pay your mortgage off completely by the time you are financially independent.**

Interest-Only Loans

Based on years of experience, I will tell you that 90% of the time choosing an interest-only loan is a poor decision because it won't require you to pay anything toward the principal. However, on selective occasions it will make sense, such as if you move frequently for work, if you know that you will only live in a house for a few years, or if you've moved to an exceptionally expensive city. Another exception is in the instance of buying a fixer-upper with the intention of spending a chunk of money on building supplies for remodeling before flipping the house for a quick profit.

Nevertheless, if you are like the vast majority considering such a loan because you can't afford the payments on conventional mortgages and the interest-only option allows you to obtain a bigger house for your money, don't do it. This would be a great time to remind yourself that you are a millionaire in the making. Millionaires own their homes free and clear by the time they are financially independent. Quite simply, *interest only* translates to paying *nothing* on principal. If you never pay the principal, you never own the house free and clear! Absolutely say *no* to a real estate agent who is eager to sell you a more expensive house in order to chalk up a higher commission on a larger sale.

Avoid interest only mortgages except in special circumstances.

Action Step 7: Keep your housing costs under 25% of your gross income, and pay off your mortgage before you retire.

Chapter 8

Living in Financial Harmony with Your Partner

There's a way of transferring funds that is even faster than electronic banking. It's called marriage.

~ James Holt McGavran

Let's face it: Fighting about money is the number one cause of divorce. It absolutely blows my mind how many people get married without ever talking about money.

If you disagree on a collaborative approach to finances before you marry, the divide in your thinking will be even wider after you marry—count on it! If you can't talk about money before you get married, plan to spend plenty of time talking about it after the wedding bells toll. You can plan on escalating voices and heated "discussions" as you and your partner make your way down Financial Lane.

Fighting about money is the top cause of divorce.

Unlike many financial experts, I'm against a prenuptial agreement—but probably not for the reasons you think. My reasoning relates to the power of thoughts. Your subconscious is at work all the time, so what you think will likely become your reality. In my mind, preparing a prenuptial agreement is tantamount to planning for divorce.

Premarital Financial Planning

I suggest a more positive way to deal with financial matters: premarital financial planning. Replacing the prenuptial agreement with a premarital financial plan will put you on the right track. In fact, I believe so strongly in this concept that I'd recommend postponing your wedding until you can come to a meeting of the minds on money. If you need a reality check, talk with anyone who is divorced. You'll find that many of them wish they had realized how expensive it is to unwind a marriage that doesn't work.

The premarital financial plan contains six crucial elements, and the success of the plan hinges on both parties truly agreeing on each element.

The six elements include the following:

1. A spending plan.
2. A plan on becoming free of any existing debt.
3. A saving plan with definitive goals for emergencies, retirement, and college funds for any children you might have.
4. A tithing or charitable donation plan.
5. An allowed debt plan, spelling out what debt you will incur, the amount of that debt, under which circumstances the debt will be allowed, and a repayment schedule.
6. A childcare plan covering who will stay home when a baby arrives, and for how long.

Now that you've decided the premarital talk about finances will take place, where do you start? First, take time to review Chapter Two. Confiding with your partner, share what you heard about money as a child. In turn, openly listen as your partner does the same. Children get most of their information from trusted adults who are seen as authorities on everything from what to eat to what to become one day. Consequently, even as an adult, you will consciously or subconsciously hold attitudes about money that are colored by your childhood teachings.

Next, talk to your partner about the effect your elders' opinions have on you now, and then sit back and listen to what your partner has to say. Truly understand why each of you thinks as you do.

Most importantly, move on and talk about what you want to create together. Paint a visual picture of the role you want money to play in your life together. Then put a plan in place to make it happen.

> **Talk about the role you want money to play in your life together, then put a plan in place to make it happen.**

As I touched on earlier, I actually had a chance to practice what I preach about this in 1992, when I married Jerry.

Here was my financial situation:

- I had no debt other than a $50,000 mortgage.
- I used automatic deductions to move money from my checking account to my investment account every month.
- I was giving 10% of my income to charity.
- I adhered to a written spending plan.

Jerry, on the other hand, had a financial picture that looked like this:

- He had an $180,000 mortgage.
- He was saving no money.

- He borrowed money every month to pay his bills, hoping that he'd get an annual bonus to pay off the debt.
- He had significant debts to repay, plus alimony payments.
- He was not giving much money to charity.
- He had no spending plan.

Essentially, he was clueless as to where his money was going. We spent many long hours talking about a debt repayment plan, a savings plan, a commitment to give to charity (tithing), and especially a spending plan. I told him that if he was not committed to sticking to the financial plan, we shouldn't get married.

I love a happy ending! Jerry agreed to all stipulations, and neither of us will ever forget the day when we were finally clear of debt (other than the mortgage). It truly was a feeling of being released from bondage.

I can report that we have had hardly any disagreements about money in our fourteen years of marriage. Admittedly, we disagreed on one issue during our first year of marriage: how much Jerry spent on clothes. We had settled on a certain amount for him to spend, but then he spent his full year's budget within a few months. He was about to buy more clothes when I pointed out that he had said he would stick to the spending plan, and he had already spent his clothing allowance for the year. He told me I was crazy, that there was no way he could have spent that amount so quickly!

Because I was tracking everything on Quicken, I could show him in less than two minutes every single purchase he had made the entire year. He truly was flabbergasted. This highlights exactly why using a spending plan is critical! Only when he saw every detail in writing did he truly realize the degree to which he was spending. His conclusion, of course, was that he needed a higher allowance for clothing! Pointing out the fixed amount of money coming in, I asked what category he wanted to reduce to keep us on track with our spending plan.

> **Only when you see every detail in writing can you truly understand how much you are spending.**

Different Strokes for Different Folks

As many different types of couples exist, numerous ways to manage your money exist as well. What matters is that you find a system that works for you. Consistency is the key. Here are two examples of money management systems that might work for you:

Example One:

Some couples keep all money in separate accounts. They create a common pool of funds in a third account to which they both contribute for joint expenses. For example, if one person earns $50,000 annually and the other earns $30,000, the first partner might contribute $20,000 to the pool, while the second gives $10,000. The pooled funds can be used for house-related expenses, groceries, and joint vacations. Each person keeps the remainder of the non-contributed funds for his or her own personal use.

Example Two:

In this scenario, all money goes into a common account with each partner taking out an equal "allowance" to pay for clothes, lunches away from home, entertainment with friends, gifts, separate travel, books, music, and personal grooming. This is the system my husband and I use. It's especially equitable if one partner has taken a career timeout for an important reason, such as continuing education or raising children full time.

Ultimately, I believe everyone should have his or her own spending money. You're asking for trouble if both of you must agree on every single purchase.

> **Everyone should have his or her own spending money.**

What about debt each of you have prior to the marriage? Again, the important thing is to have an agreement you both believe is fair and appropriate. If you are using the first system above, you probably would agree to pay off your individual debt with the money you kept for yourself after your contribution to the joint account. If you used the second example, then you would probably use the joint money to pay off the debt.

Debt will put more pressure on marital harmony than anything else. You *must* get out of debt if you want money to be a source of happiness. If you have debt, achieving your financial goals will be a distant dream. But when you are debt-free, those goals will come into focus and become reality for you.

Picking a Financial "Driver"

To keep your collaborative financial engine humming, you'll need to decide who does what. This allocation of financial responsibilities is another area that should be decided before the wedding.

Appoint the person who best handles finances, and the other person can contribute equally by taking on other types of chores. In my household, for example, I handle 100% of the financial chores because I enjoy them and am good at it. Jerry does not at all enjoy dealing with the finances, so he is thrilled that I remove the responsibility from his shoulders. Instead, Jerry agreed to handle the grocery shopping and kitchen cleanup as the tradeoff. We each think we gained the better end of the bargain, so that's a win-win situation!

Because a number of financial tasks are to be considered, I've provided you with a comprehensive list. To advance toward financial harmony, consider each of the following ten questions and then allocate the financial responsibilities based on partner skill sets. Remember, no answer is right or wrong.

- Who pays the bills?
- Who handles the routine banking (making deposits, getting cash from the ATM, balancing the checkbook, etc.)?

- Who monitors any credit card spending (making sure you have no erroneous charges; entering the spending into the budget; paying the bill each month, etc.)?
- Who monitors the progress on paying down debt and building up net worth?
- Who performs the investment research and then monitors the investment performance?
- Who keeps track of the investments (original cost, current value, etc.)?
- Who tracks what is spent on the spending plan?
- Who reviews the insurance and keeps it up-to-date?
- Who prepares the tax returns?
- Who handles the estate planning (preparation and periodic updates of wills, trusts, and powers of attorney)?

If you both dislike doing any or all of the above, then several options are available. One is to take turns, alternating once each quarter or each year, or any time frame that works for you. Another is to hire someone to accomplish most of the tasks for you. The final option is to negotiate a tradeoff: One of you agrees to take charge in exchange for the other person assuming another task you both find equally odious.

If you can't agree on who should handle the family finances, negotiate a method that works for both of you.

If one of you handles 100% of the finances, be sure to have an annual powwow to discuss financial progress and to keep the other partner in the loop. Anyone could be hit by a bus at any time, so both should know the passwords, the location of the safety deposit box, and exactly how much money and life insurance you possess.

Do yourselves a big favor by keeping an annual net worth statement in a permanent file. The statement lists everything you own, defines everything you owe, and calculates the difference. On the days when finances seem to be getting the better of you, you can gain encouragement. Reviewing your statements will remind you of how your net worth continues to grow each year.

> **Keeping an annual net worth statement will remind you of the progress you are making.**

My experience shows that couples who take the time to follow the suggestions from this chapter are successful in managing their money. However, if you somehow continue fighting about money after following every recommendation, please seek help. An older couple you both respect would be an excellent choice to enlist in helping to achieve financial agreement. Or perhaps you could consult a counselor at your church, temple, or mosque. Another option would be to hire a professional counselor, a financial planner, or even a professional mediator. Do whatever it takes! For your marriage to grow and thrive, you must see eye to eye.

> **If you want your marriage to grow and thrive, you must see eye to eye on money. Seek help if you still fight after following these suggestions.**

If You Go Your Separate Ways

In my former marriage, we had a premarital financial plan, but the marriage did not succeed. Nevertheless, the plan helped us save money when we divorced. I also believe that our plan spared us a great deal of the emotional cost that most divorces suffer.

When we decided to divorce, we were able to list all of our assets on one piece of paper, agree on the value of each asset, and then divide it into a fair 50/50 split. The entire process took less than 10 minutes! We agreed that it was crazy to waste money on divorce attorneys, so we wrote up our own agreement. We hired one attorney to translate our agreement into legalese, and were divorced for a total cost of $1,200.

Little bitterness resulted after our divorce, as we each felt that we had received a fair settlement. And we were both delighted that we didn't have to waste money on lawyers! Also, we had been living on one income and saving one, so when we split into two households, we were able to do so without financial strain to either party.

Jerry's divorce exemplified the exact opposite situation. He and his ex-wife racked up nearly $150,000 in divorce attorney fees (which we spent the first several years of our marriage paying off). A great deal of acrimony existed between them, with neither of them feeling the settlement was fair. I believe much of that would have been averted if they had been living on a spending plan and reviewing their finances together on a regular basis. If so, both would have known exactly how much net worth they possessed, how much cash flow existed, and exactly how much their expenses totaled. However, since they lacked a spending plan, lawyers had to submit subpoenas to determine each number. What an expensive way to accomplish a spending plan!

> **Not only can you save money by handling your own property division, but you will also likely experience less bitterness after the divorce.**

If you find yourself in the unfortunate situation of divorcing and then disagreeing on what is a fair settlement, consider hiring a professional mediator rather than two lawyers. The cost will be far less. Furthermore, you can complete the divorce with significantly less ill will toward one another if you haven't been battling it out through lawyers for months or years.

To find a mediator, contact your county's Alternative Dispute Resolution office for a list of the trained professionals in your area. Be sure to interview several different people over the phone, asking about their education and training, and determining the percentage of the cases they have handled with successful outcomes. You will want to choose the person with whom you are most comfortable, someone who can help you both come to a fair settlement without resorting to fighting it out with two expensive lawyers.

> **If you divorce, consider hiring a professional mediator rather than two lawyers.**

In every good marriage, the partners need to work together toward common goals, and that point is especially true when dealing with finances.

Action Step 8: Do premarital financial planning and then work together to handle all of the necessary financial tasks.

Chapter 9
The Power of Tithing

There are three kicks in every dollar. One when you make it. One when you save it. One when you give it away. And the last is the biggest of all.

~ William Allen White

At the age of 38, I was contributing about $25 per week to my church and another $300 per year to other charities. I thought I was being generous. The amount represented less than 3% of my income at the time, although that rate put me above the national average for charitable giving.

Three months after my divorce, a friend loaned me some recordings that talked about the power of giving away money (tithing). When the authors suggested donating 10% of my gross income, I nearly flipped! Triple the amount of my gifts? Sure, that may have been possible prior to the divorce, when we were saving almost 50% of our income. Now I was happy just to save 10% and stay out of debt. The thought of giving away 7% more was almost unfathomable.

Give Some Money Away

Ultimately, whether or not you can give much money to others in need comes down to your personal beliefs about the world. Believing that a power greater than yourself is running the universe puts a completely different spin on the world. With belief in a higher power comes the belief that good is rewarded.

Such thinking is a leap of faith for many, which I suppose is why believing in a higher power is faith! I've chosen a tricky topic of discussion, as it is obviously spiritual rather than scientific, and not everyone thinks alike. But from my own experience and the experiences of many of my friends and clients, I am compelled to share a process that works every time.

Quite simply, if you put good into the universe, good will come back to you. As I look over my life since the point 19 years ago at which I regularly began giving away at least 10% of my income, I can see that what I gave came back to me multifold. The ratio varies, and the reward doesn't typically occur when you expect it, but it does happen.

If you put good into the universe, good will come back to you.

The best example came about two years after Jerry and I were married. As I mentioned, he had a heavy load of debt to pay off, and he had not been donating much money to good causes before we married. But we agreed to give away 10% of our income while adhering to our specific debt repayment plan.

When writing down our cash flow numbers, I had estimated that paying off the debt would take about five years. Instead, we were free of debt in just over two years, even while making charitable donations. We were flabbergasted, but why should we be? Jerry was living within a written spending plan for the first time in over 30 years, which effectively curbed his spending. What we did not count on was his dramatic growth in income. Was that coincidence? Maybe it was. But I can point to several other financial factors that worked in our favor—far more to our advantage than we ever expected—that I honestly do not believe were mere "coincidences" occurring one after another.

The series of events certainly reinforced our faith. A few years after we were free of debt, a large national corporation acquired Jerry's company. His stock in his closely held company was not worth much at the time he had divorced, but when the business was acquired, we received about 15 times the book value of the stock. In other words, stock we had thought was worth $1 sold for $15. The difference between what we had believed the stock was worth and what its actual selling price was amounted to 10% of our income for many years!

Additionally, between 2002 and 2006, Jerry was laid off several times and spent months searching full time for a new position. In 2005, for the first time in our lives, we were living on one income and had to cash out investments to pay a portion of our living expenses. Yet when I calculated a net worth statement (how much we owned minus how much debt we owed) at the end of the year, we still enjoyed an increase of about 15% in our net worth during the year, despite having to spend part of our investment funds for living expenses. The stock market was not up 15%, but somehow our investments were. Was that coincidence?

You'll Manage Your Money Better

If for no other reason, tithing makes a positive impact because it forces us to use a written spending plan. Most people barely make ends meet from month to month. When we decide to donate money, tracking our spending becomes all the more imperative to ensure enough is "left over."

A powerful reason that tithing makes a positive impact on personal finances is that it requires the use of a written spending plan.

I have also learned that contributing money enables us to relinquish control in a positive way. Why is this important? You have probably heard that the universe has abundance available, but its gifts flow only to those who are ready to receive them. Giving up control means that you stop believing that you control everything in your life, thereby opening yourself to the possibility that the universe—or Higher Power—might be in control. Not only do you allow yourself to relinquish a tremendously heavy burden, but you also choose to make yourself open to receiving abundance along with spiritual guidance.

Although I cannot specifically prove this idea with science, I can offer countless firsthand experiences and situations told directly to me by others which reinforce the value of giving. The payoff will not be a specified return on your investment, but I would be happy to guarantee your odds are far better than playing the lottery. Have faith!

My faith in tithing was reinforced a couple of years after my divorce when money was extremely tight. All my discretionary income at the time was paying for psychological counseling so that I could get my head together. New clothes and all other optional purchases had stopped, although I had continued with my plan of giving. So I was struggling somewhat when an old friend of mine and I decided to get together when he was visiting in Atlanta.

We thought it would be fun to go jogging. My running shoes, to put it gently, were worn out. Later, we took my car to go out to dinner, and obvious then was the fact that I had delayed some needed auto maintenance. When my friend started teasing me about it, I ended up in tears. I didn't have anything to prove to him, but I felt embarrassed to look so ratty in front of an old friend.

Meanwhile, this friend of mine had made one million dollars the previous year, at the age of 40. Interestingly, I was the one who had always told him that I knew he would be a millionaire early in life, as he was an enterprising person. He was also goodhearted. After his visit, he sent me a check for $1,000 with instructions to spend it all on new clothes and other frivolous purchases. I was not allowed to repair the car or spend the money on my kids. Was this coincidence? I had not seen him in

15 years nor have we met since. But he was there when I needed a boost. I certainly choose to believe that sending good into the universe sends good back in return.

If you feel the universe is full of abundance, you open the floodgates for more to flow back to you when you contribute 10% to causes you believe are worthy and to those less fortunate. I wholeheartedly recommend that you conduct your own survey. If the outcomes reported to you are similar to the ones I described, what have you got to lose by testing the practice yourself?

> **If you believe the universe is full of abundance, by giving more you open the floodgates to receiving more.**

Expect the Unexpected

I have heard countless stories of people taking the leap of faith in giving away money each month, even when they wondered if enough would be left to pay all of their bills and meet their savings goals. For them, giving is a joy—not a sacrifice. Below is a sample of their personal comments to me:

- When we decided to begin giving regularly, we sat down to review our spending plan and realized we could cut spending in four different areas without much trouble, easily covering our gifting.
- I started giving and then, unexpectedly, I got a new position at work, bringing not only more responsibility but also a raise of 12%.
- Right after we began tithing, I received an unexpected gift from an elderly aunt.
- A new client just began using our services after I began tithing, and our company's revenue jumped 15% overnight.
- I had been making contributions all year. At tax time, my accountant called to say she realized that we had forgotten to take a deduction, and once she corrected this for the last few years, I'd get a substantial refund.

107

- I wasn't expecting anything in return, but I just sold a car for $6,000, and I'd thought it was only worth $3,000.
- I entered a silly jingle contest on a whim, won third place, and found a check for $4,000 in my mailbox.

While giving money can deliver monetary rewards, the financial returns are truly not the main focus. The amazing feeling you will experience from donating money to help those who are in need is transforming. In truth, your heart will be transformed. I am the biggest living proof of this. I was stingy 20 years ago, begrudging almost all of the money I gave away. I felt like I *had* to, while rarely did I *want* to. Not long after I began tithing, my heart completely changed.

> **The good you do is always returned at some point, either in adding tangible financial returns or in increasing your happiness and broadening your heart.**

After my husband had been unemployed for a long while, we determined that we needed to cut back on our giving; because he wasn't working, the percentage of our typical contributions amounted to significantly more than 10% of our gross income. As the year drew to a close, we were not able to write the usual substantial year-end checks. We felt terrible. During the year, we had spent little on clothes, restaurants, vacations, and other luxuries. We both agreed that we didn't particularly miss the perks, but we did miss writing our generous checks to support the people and causes that are important to us. Talk about a change of heart!

First Change Your Actions

Changing the way you feel and think is a fascinating process. You may have heard that what we create for ourselves is based on our thoughts, our words, and our actions. Generally, your words reflect your thoughts and beliefs about something. The actions you then take are usually consistent with your beliefs and your words. If you want to change something you don't like in your life, you have to change your beliefs. If you change your beliefs, the words and actions will follow.

How, then, do we go about changing beliefs, which are often ingrained since babyhood? The two methods I offer may seem counterintuitive, but they most certainly do work. One is to change your words. Even if what you say is quite different from what you believe, if you speak the words you wish to believe often, saying them with positive feelings, eventually your beliefs will change. We refer to such statements as *affirmations*, and they have changed the lives of many.

The second method, which is even more powerful, is to change your actions. Let's assume you believe that you can barely make it from paycheck to paycheck. Giving, therefore, appears nowhere on your radar screen. With not enough money for your own needs, how can you possibly give away any? You believe this to be true. Nevertheless, by making donations despite that belief, you also make the decision to trust God or the universe to take care of you. Your actions indicate a leap of faith and, eventually, a change in belief.

> **One quick way to change your belief is simply to change your action. Start giving money away now.**

To change your thinking even more quickly, start giving money away while also repeating empowering affirmations. I repeat my own affirmations several times each day. Some may seem downright hokey: *I now receive large sums of money, just for being me!* But guess what? They work! They also make me laugh, which always feels terrific. If you believe in the law of attraction, then you already know that when you are happy and feeling good, the positive energy flowing from you will attract a flow of good into your life.

> **To change your thinking even more quickly, give money away while also repeating empowering affirmations.**

Some might say that the law of attraction is supernatural. However, from a purely logical perspective, we can observe the consequences of a person's thoughts. Most bosses, for instance, prefer to promote the employee who smiles and maintains a cheerful outlook versus the one who constantly frowns with worry. Therefore, taking actions which make you happier changes your overall attitude. A cheerful attitude leads to positive expectations, which are felt by those around you. In turn, optimism influences confident action. The cycle perpetuates, inspiring continued steps in the right direction with more positive consequences, all reinforcing a positive outlook and disposition.

Whether you opt for the scientific approach or whether you choose to have faith, I would like to share a story about two people discussing whether God existed. Neither could be sure of the answer. Still, one decided that he would believe in God because if he was wrong, the belief would not worsen his condition. To the contrary, he knew he would be far happier. First, he could trust that God would bring wonderful things into his life. Second, he would delegate the burden of his fears, worries and concerns to God. For certain, he would never have fears or worries about money!

Action Step 9: Trust that the universe and God are good; give money to charity with a cheerful, confident spirit.

Chapter 10

Introduction to Investments

Rule No.1: Never lose money. Rule No.2: Never forget rule No.1.

~ Warren Buffett

The clients in my financial planning practice have $200,000 or more in investments that I manage for them. I recently raised this to $500,000 for new clients, and my associates now handle the clients with less. I established a higher minimum because my time only allows me to perform a topnotch job for one hundred clients or fewer. Since my expenses per client average more than $1,000 and my investment management fee is 1% of the assets under management, working with a client with only $50,000 to invest would cause me to generate a loss. Thus, we set a minimum investment account size of $200,000. Such a practice is typical in my profession.

How does this affect you? Small investors should be forewarned that most financial advisors who work with small accounts do so because they are just starting out and are still working to establish a practice. I don't know about you, but when it comes to my financial future, I wouldn't want to let someone practice with my money. Should you ever need an investment advisor, I highly recommend looking for someone with at least 10 years of experience. Most who are new to the profession don't know much more about investing than you do.

Rather than taking risks with an inexperienced advisor, you would be better off opening a self-directed account at E*TRADE, TD Ameritrade, Schwab, or one of the other online broker dealers. You might also consider opening an account at Vanguard, Fidelity, or another big mutual fund family. Don't let someone train to become an expert while making mistakes with your money!

I'm proud to tell you that I'm an investment expert, but reaching that status didn't happen overnight. It took many years of work and plenty of mistakes, and I am now an excellent investor—primarily because I learned from all of those mistakes!

The sole purpose of the next two chapters is to teach you about the mistakes I made so you can learn to be a good investor faster without making quite so many errors. The concepts are basic and intended for those who are just getting started. The tips you'll learn here will also enable you to handle your own investments until you have accumulated enough capital to hire a good investment manager, or until you have become skilled yourself. If you happen to be an experienced investor who wants to learn more, you can find hundreds of investment books on the market that will delve into greater detail.

You *can* learn to become an excellent investor, but you have to give yourself some room to make a few mistakes. No matter how many books you read or how many classes you attend, you *will* make mistakes. Just be sure to learn from them, as any expert does.

> **Don't let someone train to become a financial expert by making mistakes with your money. Instead, train yourself, making your own mistakes and learning from them.**

Start with an Emergency Fund

For those of you who are saving money and making progress in cleaning up your debt, good for you! Give yourself a big pat on the back. Now is the time to decide what to do with the money you've saved. Will it be a 401(k), Roth IRA, or other financial independence vehicle?

The first step you want to take is to build an emergency fund of cash to be available at a moment's notice. You'd be amazed at the number of people who have no emergency fund. Don't be in that group.

Of course, in choosing to create an emergency fund, you need to figure out how much money it should contain. Opinions vary. Some recommend three months' worth of expenses, some advocate six months' worth, some suggest a year's worth. Initially, I suggest that you shoot for an amount to cover three months of expenses. (This is the amount I mentioned when we discussed spending plans.) Establishing a goal that seems achievable is preferable to creating one that is so high that you will not attempt to meet it.

Save at least three months' worth of expenses in an emergency fund.

You'll next need to determine where the money will be held. The two most typical places to put this money are in a savings account at your bank or credit union, or in a money market account. You can open the money market account with your bank, a mutual fund company, or one of the various companies located on the Internet. We'll discuss mutual fund companies in just a moment. For now, simply know that these are your choices.

How do you choose which option is best? First, look at the interest rate that each source offers. Ideally, you want to choose the one with the highest interest rate. However, if your savings are small, say $500, the difference between 3% interest and 4% interest is only $5 per year. In that case, you might make your decision based on convenience, such as keeping your checking and savings accounts at the same bank. Although some Internet institutions pay higher interest rates, they might present some inconveniences to use.

The second consideration in selecting an account is whether any restrictions will exist to accessing the money. For example, some accounts allow a limited number of transactions per month or per quarter. Others might charge a fee for each transaction or withdrawal. Others might require a minimum balance or make you forfeit the interest earned if you don't keep the money there for a certain specified period.

If you perform an Internet search using "high interest savings" as the key words, you will find dozens of business websites. A good general site is www.bankrate.com, which will display interest rates at many different banks. Because interest rates change frequently, base your choice on a current search. As of this writing, three sites that offer especially high returns are www.eloan.com, www.emigrantdirect.com, and www.direct. citibank.com.

Home Equity Line of Credit

Homeowners who are truly disciplined with their money have another option to consider. *Truly disciplined* means you carry no debt other than a mortgage, you are currently saving at least 10% every single month, and you pay off your credit cards in full every single month. *Absolutely* disciplined means you'd rather eat dirt than pay interest you don't *absolutely* have to pay.

If you fall within this category, you might contemplate opening a home equity line of credit (HELOC). This line of credit from a bank or mortgage company allows you to borrow from the equity in your home. Again, equity is the value of your home minus the current mortgage debt. The bank will file a second mortgage on your home, which provides collateral for the HELOC.

The advantage of a HELOC is that you can borrow cash at a moment's notice, pay it back whenever you want to, and only pay interest on the loan when you have a balance outstanding. The disadvantage is that if you don't pay the loan as agreed, the bank can foreclose on your home in order to obtain the money to pay off your debt. For this reason, I emphasize only using a HELOC if you are truly disciplined with your money.

Only use a home equity line if you are extremely disciplined with your money.

I personally use a HELOC since I can't stand to have my money earning only 3- 4% a year in a money market account. Therefore, I keep all of my cash invested in mutual funds, and if an emergency arises, I can use my HELOC for quick cash. During the last 30 years, I have faced only two occasions when I had true emergencies requiring immediate cash. Both times I was able to pay the line of credit back quickly. So for me, keeping my money invested in mutual funds has been more beneficial than keeping emergency funds in a money market account.

Again, a home equity line of credit is a recommendation for those of you who are running a tight financial ship. If you have unpaid credit card balances or other consumer debt, a HELOC is not for you.

While we are on the subject of HELOCs, let me answer a question I hear frequently: Should you use a HELOC to pay off your credit cards, your car loan, or other consumer debt? My answer: *Never!* The reason should be logical. If you have credit card or consumer debt in the first place, you have been spending in advance—spending more than you are earning.

Never use a home equity line to consolidate your consumer debt.

If you have been spending more than you earn, please don't consider a HELOC as an option. Statistics show that most people who consolidate their debt end up borrowing more. The odds predict that a year or two from now, in addition to the HELOC debt, you will also have added new consumer debt.

If you have been spending in advance of earning, running up balances on credit cards or consumer loans, you simply must retrain yourself. Break that habit. You will accomplish the task only by putting yourself through the pain of paying off that debt! When a person maps out a plan to become rid of debt, following the schedule month after month until it's paid off, he or she is much less likely to slide back into debt in the future. The pain is enough to remind someone not to repeat the mistake ever again!

What happens, then, if you consolidate the debt into the HELOC? You suffer no pain. For most, without pain no lesson is learned. I must reiterate: Use a HELOC *only* if you are one of those exemplary folks who has no consumer debt, and you save religiously!

Investing in Mutual Funds

Once you have put aside three months' worth of living expenses for emergencies, I recommend investing in mutual funds. Here's an illustration of a mutual fund: Imagine a pot sits in the center of a room among hundreds of people (you and I included) who want to invest money. We decide that we'd like to invest in the stock market because it offers rates of return that are much higher, on average, than what we could earn on CDs (certificates of deposit), savings accounts, or money market funds. The problem is that we don't know how to conduct the research necessary to determine in which companies we should invest. Should we invest in Coca-Cola? Disney? A small company that's unfamiliar to most? And if we buy this stock, when should we sell it?

Because we are not trained investors, we decide to hire a professional money manager to determine which stocks to purchase. Trained to know which stocks to buy, our money manager will be in charge of deciding which companies to invest in, when to buy in, and when to sell out. We then each put our share of money into the pot. In doing so, we have created a mutual fund.

> **A mutual fund is a "pot" of money shared among investors who employ a professional manager to buy and sell investments on their behalf.**

A mutual fund, then, is simply a "pot" of shared money with hundreds, thousands, or even millions of investors. Each mutual fund has a professional money manager whose job it is to buy and sell the investments in the portfolio. The investors have to pay the mutual fund company a fee, called *the expense ratio,* to hire the portfolio manager and the researchers who provide the necessary data to the portfolio manager, as well as to cover the administrative expenses and paperwork costs associated with the record keeping.

If you have invested in mutual funds before, then you know that hundreds of different types exist. Momentarily, I'll provide an overview of some of the major categories of mutual funds.

Investing in Stocks

What is a *stock?* Stock represents ownership in a company. One share of stock represents one unit of ownership in a particular company. If you own 100 shares of Coca-Cola stock, you are a tiny part owner of The Coca-Cola Company. If the company performs well financially, your stock will increase in value. If the company does poorly, your stock value decreases. If the company goes bankrupt, the value of your stock may drop to a few pennies or even nothing. The value of your stock essentially fluctuates up and down in line with the company's financial performance.

> **Stock represents ownership in a company. One share of stock is equal to one unit of ownership in the company.**

Even though the risk always exists (although the risk can be teeny) that a company will go out of business, people buy stocks. Why? Historically, stock returns have yielded about 10-11% per year on average. One of the reasons I like stock mutual funds is that they tend to offer the high returns of the stock market with less risk. You see, a particular mutual fund will tend to contain the stocks of one hundred or more companies. Therefore, even if the manager picks one company that goes out of business, your ownership of that company will likely only represent 1-2% of your total holdings in the mutual fund. Such a small percentage of ownership in a company that failed probably won't hurt you. Your risk is radically lower than if you had purchased only the failed company's stock.

I always recommend to my clients that they invest a healthy portion of their money into stock mutual funds because history has shown that stocks tend to average more than 10% in the long run. However, investing in stocks can be risky since they fluctuate in value. The biggest way to reduce your risk in stock investing is to diversify into a number of different categories of stock mutual funds.

Investing in stock mutual funds is recommended because history has shown that stocks tend to average more than 10% a year in the long run.

Some mutual funds are called *value funds*, while others are called *growth funds*. A growth company is one that is expected to grow faster than average in the coming years. Twenty years ago, companies such as Home Depot and Microsoft were considered growth companies. Generally, investors pay a premium price for investing in a company they expect to grow quickly.

A value company is generally older, more established, and, therefore, not expected to grow as fast as the average company. Often, a value company is one that has experienced trouble for one reason or another, so the earnings are no longer growing as rapidly. For this reason, investors typically pay a lower price for investing in a value company than in a growth company.

The measurement used to decide the value of the stock is called the *price/earnings ratio (P/E ratio)*. If a company is selling for $50 per share and demonstrates earnings of $1 per share, then the company's price/earnings ratio (P/E ratio) is 50/1, or 50. A stock that is selling for $50 a share, while the earnings are $10 a share, has a P/E ratio of 50/10, or 5. The company with a 50 P/E would be a growth stock, while the company with the P/E of 5 would be a value stock.

Why would you care about the P/E ratio on a stock? The P/E ratio provides a simple measuring stick to gauge whether the price of a stock is reasonable. For example, let's assume 20 years ago you were deciding whether to buy Home Depot or Microsoft stock. In my made-up example, let's further assume both companies had a P/E ratio of 40, and their stock sold for the exact same price. If you believed that Home Depot would grow faster than Microsoft, you would buy Home Depot since the P/E ratios and the stock prices were identical.

> **The P/E ratio on a stock is a simple measuring stick that allows you to gauge whether the price of a stock is reasonable.**

But suppose Home Depot's P/E was 60 (price is $60 and earnings are $1) and Microsoft's was 30 (price is $60 and earnings are $2). Would you still want to buy the Home Depot stock? The difference in the two ratios indicates that investors believe Home Depot will grow twice as fast as Microsoft (paying $60 for every $1 of earnings versus paying $60 for every $2 of earnings). If you, on the other hand, think that Home Depot will grow only 1.5 times faster than Microsoft, then you would be better off buying the Microsoft stock.

Why do we care whether a stock is a value stock or a growth stock? The primary reason is that growth and value stocks behave differently at different times in the stock market cycle. During some years, growth stocks will perform wonderfully and value stocks horribly, and vice versa. Consequently, a wise investor owns shares of each—some growth and some value. Owning different types of stock is an example of what is meant by *diversifying* your investments. Not only do you want to own different companies (therefore, different mutual funds), but you also want to have some growth funds and some value funds.

Another means of diversification involves owning large-cap funds, mid-cap funds, and small-cap funds. *Cap* means *capitalization*, or the market value of the company. Capitalization is simply the number of shares of stock outstanding, multiplied by the market value of each share. So a company that has 20 million shares outstanding and trades for $100 a share has a market cap of 20,000,000 x 100 ($2 billion). A company that has 200 million shares outstanding and trades for $140 a share has a market cap of 200,000,000 x 140 ($28 billion).

Generally, large-cap companies are extremely large corporations that everyone has heard of, such as GE, Microsoft, Coca-Cola, and Citicorp. Mid-cap companies are typically those that are well-known only in their hometown areas. Although they are often older, well-established companies, they aren't big enough to have moved into the large-cap category. A small-cap company is usually less familiar. If the company is successful and grows, it will become a mid-cap company in time. Similarly, a successful mid-cap company may grow to large-cap status.

So why should you care if a company is small cap, mid cap, or large cap? The reason again relates to portfolio diversification. Most of the time, the rate of return or investment performance will be different in any given year among the various categories. During one year, your large caps might show terrific performance, while your mid caps deliver so-so returns and your small caps yield awful results. The next year, the small caps might be fabulous, the large caps so-so, and the mid caps terrible. Most good portfolios carry a blend of some large-cap, some mid-cap, and some small-cap investments.

By combining the previous concepts, we can diversify your portfolio even more. A portfolio, for instance, can include large-cap growth funds or large-cap value funds. In fact, a good portfolio should have both. Sometimes mutual funds will be called *core* or *blend* funds. Either term generally means that the fund contains both value and growth in the same portfolio.

In addition to the size of the capitalization, you can also choose mutual funds based on whether they contain U.S. companies or companies headquartered outside the United States. As the marketplace continues to globalize, including international funds in your portfolio becomes all the more important.

Emerging market funds are a special type of international funds. Generally, such stocks are of companies which are headquartered in third-world countries. Therefore, many of the companies in Latin America or the lesser developed Far East or Eastern Europe would be considered emerging market companies. The values tend to fluctuate greatly from year to year, so investors typically will not have more than 5-10% of their portfolios invested in emerging market funds. A conservative investor will have no money in emerging market funds.

Let's now return to our room with that original pot of money. When we hire our fund manager, we give him or her exact guidelines. We might say to invest in large-cap growth companies, in mid-cap value companies, in emerging market companies, in large-cap value companies internationally, etc. The combinations are almost endless. Additionally, we want to tell our mutual fund manager to invest in either stocks or bonds, or some combination of the two.

Investing in Bonds

What is a *bond*? A bond is just a loan. Every loan has three elements: the *principal* amount (the amount borrowed), the *interest rate*, and the *maturity* date (when the loan is due). If you ask your bank to borrow money to buy a car, you might borrow $10,000, the interest might be 7.5%, and you would make monthly payments for three-five years, until you reach the maturity date.

A bond is a loan to a corporation, the government, or a municipality.

While a company can obtain a corporate loan from the bank, large, well-known companies may decide to borrow directly from the public instead, as this is often less expensive. That kind of loan would be a *corporate bond*. The principal amount will usually be offered in multiples of $1,000, an interest rate (let's say 6% for our example) will be offered, and a maturity date, or the date that the company promises to pay back the money, will be specified.

Generally in regard to bonds, all the money is paid back in one single payment at maturity. At times, regular quarterly payments will be provided, but that practice is not common. If Coca-Cola issues bonds with a 6% interest rate and promises to pay back the money in 15 years, the bond would be called a 6% 15-year corporate bond.

If the U.S. government takes out a loan, a government bond is created. The need to issue bonds usually happens when Uncle Sam is spending more than he is receiving in taxes (hence the federal deficit). Bonds are issued to make up the difference.

If Uncle Sam wants to borrow $20 billion, for example, 20-year bonds at 5% might be offered. As the investor, you can decide whether you prefer 15-year bonds with Coca-Cola at 6% or 20-year bonds with the U.S. government at 5%. Generally, companies must pay higher interest rates than the U.S. government since most investors are more confident that the government, as compared to a company, will still be around to repay the money at maturity.

A third category of bonds is called *municipal bonds*. A municipality is generally a local government unit, such as a city, a county, a water district, or a highway authority. A special quirk in the tax laws states that investors don't have to pay federal income taxes on municipal bonds. As a result, municipal bonds don't have to pay as high of an interest rate to entice investors. Wealthy people buy municipals to avoid federal income taxes. Generally, if you buy a bond in the state in which you live, you won't have to pay state income taxes either. Therefore, a benefit usually exists in purchasing municipal bonds issued in your own state.

It's important to note that not all bonds are created equally because the entities issuing the bonds are not equal. For instance, most people would rather invest in a bond with Coca-Cola than with Delta Air Lines (two examples of companies based in my hometown of Atlanta). Because Delta has filed for bankruptcy, the company possibly won't exist in 15-20 years. A person would take a higher risk loaning money to such a corporation.

Have you heard of *junk bonds*? Companies or municipalities that are experiencing financial difficulties have issued such bonds, which represent high risk since the issuers may be unable to repay the bondholders. As the name indicates, such bonds could be worthless. Not surprisingly, if you buy a junk bond, you should receive a higher interest rate or higher yield for the risk you take.

Some people think *high-yield bonds* are the same as junk bonds, but actually they are different—and the distinction is important. When a company decides to expand to build a new plant, for example, in order to obtain the necessary funds, it will raise the money by taking a bank loan, issuing bonds or by selling more stock. Sometimes rapidly growing smaller companies issue bonds to borrow the money needed to grow, rather than issuing new stock. They are called *high-yield bonds* because the smaller, unknown companies must offer higher interest rates to tempt people to loan the money to the company.

For example, Coca-Cola might be able to raise money with a 7% bond because everyone knows about the company. Also, most believe Coke will pay off the debt. However, if the unknown XYZ Company chooses to issue bonds to raise money, it might have to offer 10%, 11% or 12% to entice investors to take a risk on an unknown company.

What, then, is the essential difference between a junk bond and a high-yield bond? A *junk bond* is owed by a company that is having financial difficulty and, therefore, carries a high risk of not being able to pay back the debt. Conversely, *a high-yield bond* may be issued by a healthy company that must pay a premium interest rate because the corporate name is unfamiliar to the general public.

Most people believe that bonds are far safer than stocks in that their value will not fluctuate as stocks do. This perception may or may not be true. Generally, the point is true for a *short-term bond* (meaning the bond will mature and repay your principal in a few years) that is issued by a strong company, municipality, or the U.S. government. However, if a bond is issued by a company that runs into financial trouble (remember junk bonds?), then the business may not be able to repay your principal to you at maturity. Or it may pay only part of what is due.

More importantly, bonds have interest rate risk. In general, when interest rates go up, bond values go down, and vice versa. The longer the term of the bond, the more its value will be affected by changes in interest rates. To make this crystal clear, I will give you an example:

> **Most people believe that bonds are far safer than stocks in that they don't fluctuate in value as much as stocks. The perception may or may not be true.**

Let's say that you buy a bond for $1,000. This one pays interest of 5%, or $50 a year, for the next 20 years, and repays your principal of $1,000 in 20 years. Suppose that interest rates rise to 7% a year after you purchase the first bond. You buy another 20-year bond for $1,000. This one will pay you 7%, or $70 a year, for the next 20 years, and then repay your initial $1,000.

Meanwhile, an emergency arises, and you must raise $2,000 quickly. You come to me and say, "Jan, please buy my two bonds from me for $2,000." I will look at current bond prices. If I see that I could buy a new bond for $1,000 that would pay me 7% a year for the next 20 years, I'd be delighted to buy your second bond for the same $1,000.

However, would I want to buy your first bond that pays only $50 a year if I could buy a new bond that would pay me $70 a year? Of course not! You could sell your 5% bond to me only by selling it for less than $1,000. Maybe I would pay you around $700, with the exact amount determined by a formula that makes the value of the bond's yield equivalent to 7%. (This is why bond values go down when interest rates go up.) So if you believe that interest rates will be rising, a smart strategy is to buy only short-term bonds.

Historically, bond yields have been around 6% or 7% per year. Returns on bonds from 1980 to 2006 have been much higher, around 9%. The reason is that interest rates declined from over 21% in 1980 down to about 2% in 2004. Remember that when interest rates are falling, bond prices are rising.

Another example will further explain the point. Assume you bought a $1,000-bond in 1981 with an interest rate of 18%. You would earn $180 a year in interest, plus your $1,000 principal is repaid at maturity. Five years later, if interest rates had fallen to 11%, a new bond would pay only $110 per year. If you decided to sell your old bond that paid $180 per year, you will be able to sell it for more than $1,000 since the buyer would continue to receive those higher interest payments for the life of the bond. Therefore, when interest rates declined, your bond value went up.

A question remains: Why buy bonds if the return on them is less than the return on stocks? Terrific question! First, bonds offer excellent diversification for your investment portfolio. Remember, stocks go up and down in value. If you look at the S&P 500 index over the last 80 years, you will see that this stock index was up an average of three of every four years, and down (lost money) about one of every four years. Quite often, if the stock market is down, the bond market will be doing well. Thus, if some of your money is invested in bonds, yet the stock market goes down one year, at least part of your portfolio will be earning positive returns.

Bonds offer excellent diversification for your investment portfolio, and they are generally less volatile than stocks.

Second, the bond market is less volatile than the stock market, so the presence of bonds in your portfolio can make your returns steadier than if you had an all-stock portfolio. A bad year in the bond market might produce negative returns of 3-10%, while a bad year in the stock market might show negative returns of 10-30%, as an example. If all your money is in the stock market, your returns look similar to a roller-coaster ride: up some of the time and down some of the time. If you have part of your money in bonds, the roller coaster ride will be gentler, as the ups and downs are not nearly as drastic.

The most crucial point about investing, which I teach all of my clients, is that the stock market goes up and it goes down. You need to know this fact in advance and plan on it. Therefore, when you have a down year in the stock market, tell yourself that the occurrence is normal and wait for the trend to change. The biggest mistake many investors make is selling when the market is declining (selling low) and buying when the market has been skyrocketing (buying high). If you are one of the smart ones who buys low and sells high, you will do quite well as an investor.

> **The most crucial point about investing is that the market goes up and it goes down. You need to know this fact in advance and plan on it.**

Other Investments

Real estate is another common investment. The best place to start as a real estate investor is by buying a home or a condo. Later, you may want to obtain some rental property, such as a house or condo, that you own and rent to someone else.

Many people want to own real estate investments but do not have the time or the interest to own a rental property. If that describes you, a *REIT*, or *real estate investment trust*, is a good alternative way to invest in real estate. A REIT is similar to a mutual fund. Many people contribute money to a common pool, and a professional real estate manager selects properties to purchase and manages the properties on behalf of the investors.

A REIT might own anywhere from a dozen properties to hundreds of properties, depending on how large it is.

You can own many other investments, such as oil and gas, commodities, hedge funds, venture capital, and options. If you are new as an investor, pass on these for now. Start with a solid foundation of mutual funds (both stocks and bonds, and possibly REITS) and wait until you are well-established as an investor before trying some of the more advanced investments.

Action Step 10: Be wise about investing by employing good asset allocation and good diversification.

Chapter 11

Choosing Your Investments

It's not the bulls and bears you need to avoid – it's the bum steers.

~ Chuck Hillis.

Investment Steps

Now that you understand some of the terminology and types of investments, you are ready to invest. Here are the steps to follow:

1. Determine your risk tolerance.
2. Decide on your asset allocation.
3. Decide between index mutual funds or specific funds.
4. Choose your mutual funds.
5. Choose among A shares, B shares, C shares, or no-load shares.
6. Decide whether the money will be in your 401(k), 403(b), a Roth IRA, or in personal investments.
7. Learn the reasons to avoid using annuities as an investment (save these until you are over 50 years old).

8. Learn how to choose a financial advisor if you don't want to go it alone.

One by one, we will dive in and look at each of these steps.

Risk Tolerance

Risk tolerance indicates how risky you want your investments to be. A conservative investor has a low-risk appetite, not caring for investments that fluctuate in value or present the chance of losing money. This type of investor would likely choose bank certificates of deposit (CDs) and perhaps fixed annuities and bonds, with little or no stock investments. Such an investor would prefer value stocks to growth stocks and large-cap stocks to small-cap stocks since the former in both cases fluctuates less in value from year to year.

A person with a moderate-risk appetite might be willing to tolerate some fluctuations in value of his or her investments, understanding that over the long term, the investments that fluctuate up and down will ultimately average higher returns than fixed-income investments, such as bonds or CDs. A moderate-risk investor would likely own a portfolio that includes stocks and bonds, as well as real estate investments. The higher the percentage of stocks and the lower the percentage of bonds, the riskier the portfolio will be.

An aggressive risk appetite reflects those who are willing to tolerate much larger fluctuations in value in the belief that they will enjoy much higher returns on their investments over the long term. Extremely aggressive investors will hold little if anything in the way of conservative investments, such as bonds or CDs, and will instead carry a variety of riskier investments. In addition to stocks, they might have hedge funds, commodities (gold, for example), real estate, oil and gas, and perhaps options.

A number of investment websites offer quizzes that allow you to evaluate your risk appetite. The same is true of many companies that offer 401(k) plans. For those who have already invested, simply take the "pillow test." When you put your head on the pillow at night, do you think your investments are too conservative? Do you regret your choices, feeling that you should be making more money? Or do you worry that you are too aggressive and, therefore, might lose money? Perhaps you drift off to sleep thinking, *ah, just right!* Your investment mix is wrong until you can lay your head on the pillow and feel it is "just right."

Take the pillow test to help determine your risk appetite.

Asset Allocation

Asset allocation refers to the mix of investments in your portfolio. For starters, you want to decide how much of your assets are to be in stocks, how much in bonds, how much in cash, and how much in other investment categories such as real estate, oil and gas, commodities, or hedge funds. Knowing your risk tolerance will drive your asset allocation. Those who are conservative will want mostly conservative investments, and vice versa.

The primary issue to remember with asset allocation is that no good or bad, right or wrong category exists. Strive for a mix that represents a good match for your risk appetite. I would suggest, however, that you include at least seven different categories so that no single category represents more than 15% of your total portfolio.

Have at least seven different asset categories so that no single category represents more than 15% of your total portfolio.

Let's look at some examples of asset allocation for various risk appetites.

Conservative:
Cash (CDs)	15%
Short-term bonds	15%
Intermediate-term bonds	10%
High-yield bonds	5%

Fixed annuity	15%
Conservative allocation fund	15%
Moderate allocation fund	15%
Large-cap value stocks	10%

Moderate:

Cash (CDs)	5%
Short-term bonds	10%
High-yield bonds	10%
Large-cap growth stock	10%
Large-cap value stock	15%
Mid-cap stocks	10%
Small-cap stocks	10%
International stocks	15%
Moderate allocation stocks	15%

Aggressive:

Short-term bonds	5%
High-yield bonds	5%
Large-cap growth stock	15%
Large-cap value stock	15%
Mid-cap stock	10%
Small-cap stock	10%
International stock	15%
Emerging market stock	5%
Real estate	10%
Gold	5%
Oil and gas	5%

You have probably realized by now that I love mutual funds! I have found them to be "the greatest thing since sliced bread" for several reasons. To do a good job of choosing one specific stock, you need to spend about six hours researching it. Unless picking stocks is your hobby, you consider it your passion, and you are willing to invest the time to carry out the task effectively, choose mutual funds.

I highly recommend mutual funds.

Index Funds

An *index mutual fund* is one that mimics a specific index. If you decide, for example, that you would like to have 10% of your portfolio in mid-cap stocks, a simple way to accomplish this would be to choose a mid-cap index mutual fund. Such a fund would contain a variety of mid-cap companies, each selected to mimic or imitate a mid-cap index.

Alternatively, you can choose a specific *mid-cap mutual fund*. Here, rather than having a variety of mid-cap companies that are representative of a mid-cap index, you would own perhaps one hundred specific mid-cap companies that have been chosen by the mutual fund manager because she or he believes that the companies will outperform the others.

It seems logical that you would want to pick a specific mutual fund since the manager selects the companies that are likely to outperform. However, in this case, you still may want to pick an index fund. First, the index fund should have a much lower expense ratio since the manager just mimics an index and does not have to spend any money on research or company monitoring. For example, if you buy an S&P 500 index fund, then your mutual fund will have the same 500 companies that are in the S&P 500, in the same ratio as they are in the index. If the expense ratio is .6% cheaper every year because of the absence of research and monitoring expenses, the savings can add up to a significant difference in performance over time.

Second, many mutual funds under-perform the index funds. If you lack experience or don't have the time and the interest to select superior mutual funds, picking an index fund is certainly safer than randomly picking a mutual fund. Additionally, with a specific manager at the helm, mutual funds can demonstrate a wonderful record of accomplishment. However, if the brilliant fund manager leaves, a fund with a long-running reputation of excellence can decline sharply.

Since most investors do not keep track of manager changes, you most likely would not know about a shift in control. Conversely, if you own an index fund, you never have to worry about monitoring your fund's performance or its changes in fund management.

Choose Your Mutual Funds

I'd recommend choosing index funds if you are new to investing or if you lack both the time and interest in choosing and monitoring superior mutual funds. Many index funds are available, and they are not all created equal! You could easily find five different S&P 500 index funds with five different rates of return. The differences will come from the expense ratios that each company charges—all depending upon how much of the money they take out of your fund to pay for their expenses.

> Choose index funds if you are brand new to investing or if you lack the time or interest in choosing and monitoring superior mutual funds.

I suggest going online to conduct your research. You might begin with Morningstar, a mutual fund reporting company. Other good sites include Yahoo! Finance, beginnersinvest.about.com, Fidelity Investments, Vanguard Investments, and T. Rowe Price Investments. Most online brokers, including Charles Schwab, E*TRADE, and TD Ameritrade, have terrific websites. In addition, many different financial magazines publish annual lists of the best mutual funds.

Let me issue a big caution here. When I was a brand-new investor more than 30 years ago, I would eagerly grab the list of the one hundred best mutual funds, and then run out and buy shares of the top three. Year after year, I'd lose money on these funds. What was wrong with that picture? First, I was making my decision based on the one-year returns—bad idea! Instead, choose your funds based on three-year or five-year returns.

Second, I was picking the top three and totally ignoring asset allocation. I finally learned to complete my asset allocation first, before choosing a fund for each category.

I also learned that the hot fund last year is not necessarily going to be strong next year. I needed to adjust my thinking from getting rich quickly to getting rich wisely with a well-balanced, well-thought-out portfolio.

Now that you understand asset allocation and using mutual funds to build a smart portfolio, let me give you two real-life examples of how powerful this methodology is. Both examples to follow happened recently with clients of mine.

One client is brand new. He previously worked with a broker who was buying and selling stocks. His portfolio included no asset allocation, and the broker traded the stocks he thought would be winners rather than buying mutual funds. My client *lost* $28,000 on his $1 million-portfolio over the last 3 years! In contrast, compounded returns for my clients with similar moderate-risk appetites had ranged from 10% to 14% per year for the same three-year period. The bottom line is this: $1 million growing for three years at 10% becomes $1,331,000. Growing at 14%, it becomes $1,481,544.

Another client has been with me exactly one year, and we recently conducted her first annual review. Her account has grown 12.6% over the previous 12 months. She also has money with a broker who was trading stocks in her account. Her return with him over the past year was a meager 1%. To put that in perspective with numbers, we see that $1 million growing at 12.6% annually becomes $1,126,000 after a year; $1 million at 1% grows to $1,010,000. Especially interesting about this story is the fact that she was initially reluctant to use mutual funds because her broker had told her that she would make considerably more with him since he could pick the best stocks for her.

The main point is to demonstrate that purchasing a variety of good mutual funds to achieve good and balanced asset allocation does work. Occasionally, wild times exist in the market, such as during 1998 and 1999, when picking individual "hot" stocks would move you ahead more quickly. Typically, this is a failing strategy. Still, some sophisticated investors believe mutual funds are boring. Personally, I prefer to get rich as quickly and as easily as possible, so bring on the boring mutual funds in a well-balanced portfolio!

One final note about my two clients' experiences: The returns that I cited were from 2004 to 2006. During those three years, the overall stock market was up. Please don't conclude that making a 10% to 14% return is something you could count on. Most certainly, when the stock market is down, your returns will probably be negative. My point is only to show the contrast between "boring" mutual funds and picking "hot" stocks.

Choose A, B, C or No-Load Shares

Load refers to the sales charge. If you perform your own research and pick your own funds, you always want to choose no-load shares. Why pay someone a fee to sell a mutual fund to you if you chose it yourself?

Many begin investing through their 401(k) or 403(b) plans at work. You won't typically have a choice about what share class you may buy, but if you do, always choose the C shares. Let me explain about A, B, and C shares so that you will understand the reason.

A shares have an "all in front" sales charge that is usually 4-6%. To add insult to injury, many A shares also pay a ¼% annual "trail" commission after the first year. You will rarely see A shares in a company retirement plan; however, if your retirement plan has them, run to your employer kicking and screaming, demanding that your plan be changed. You should avoid A shares at all costs!

B shares have a "back-end" sales charge. B shares are just as bad as A shares and probably worse since most people don't even realize they are subject to this charge. You won't see a sales charge when you invest. When you sell, however, a sales charge based on the number of years you have invested will be subtracted from your gains. Typically, the charge will be 5-7% the first year, declining 1% per year after that. Since the average holding period of a mutual fund is about 18 months, having B shares makes no sense to me.

I have reviewed a number of company plans using B shares. The only person who benefits from this is the salesperson who sold the plan. If you see B shares in your plan, complain to your personnel office. They are simply inappropriate.

Obviously, you want to buy no-load shares whenever possible. However, if you must pay a sales charge, *C shares* are the only way to go. Acquiring a C share will require a 1% front-end commission, with a 1% annual trail commission each year after that. Only small plans with small companies should have C shares. If the total amount in your company plan exceeds $1 million, the company should be in a position to offer *no-load* (no sales charge) shares to employees.

Obviously, you want to buy no-load shares whenever possible. However, if you must pay a sales charge, always choose C shares.

If sales fees exist in your company plan, it's usually because no one is paying attention. A company I once worked with was paying 1.65% per year in annual fees for its plan. I was able to offer less than 1% per year. The company was overpaying because no one had reviewed it in nearly a decade. Be the squeaky wheel if you see this happening in your company!

Use a 401(k), 403(b), or Roth IRA

Now that you are beginning to save money, you must decide exactly where to invest it. If your goal is to save for your eventual financial freedom, you will want to use a 401(k), 403(b), or a Roth IRA. If your company offers a plan with a matching contribution, you especially want to start there. Typically, a company will match 25 or 50 cents on the dollar, up to 6% of your income. If you contribute 6% of your income, they might contribute another 3%. Although you may elect to contribute more than 6% of your income, your company usually won't match above the 6%.

If you'd like to save more than 6% of your income (I hope you do!), then consider using a Roth IRA as well. You may contribute a certain amount per year ($4,000 in 2007 if you were under 50 years old, with that amount increasing in future years), and your investment will grow tax-free for the rest of your life. Everyone who can take advantage of Roth IRAs should leap at the opportunity. Nevertheless, since no employer will match your Roth contribution, be sure to first use a 401(k) or 403(b) if your company is matching.

If you are single and earning over $95,000 for your *adjusted gross income (or AGI)*—which is the line at the bottom of the first page of your 1040 tax return—or if you're married and earning over $150,000 AGI together, you aren't eligible for a Roth IRA. (Technically, you can invest in a partial Roth if your income is $95,000-$105,000 for a single person or $150,000-$160,000 for a married couple, but we won't go into the details here.) If you fall in this high-income category, you may want to put more than 6% into your company-sponsored plan despite the absence of matching.

Ultimately, if your future goal is to have enough money to live comfortably on your investments, you need to plan to contribute about 10% of your income for about 30 years. If you cannot contribute to a Roth IRA, put a full 10% into your company plan, even if matching past 6% isn't offered.

If your company has no plan at all, then take advantage of a Roth IRA if you are under the aforementioned limits. If you are above these income limits, then establish a traditional IRA. A traditional IRA will allow you to take a tax deduction the year of your contribution, but you will have to pay income tax on the money when you withdraw it. Both you and your spouse can contribute to your own IRAs, even if the second spouse is not working outside the home. If IRA contributions are less than 10% of your income, I recommend also beginning a personal investment account funded with mutual funds.

If your savings goals are targeted for something other than financial freedom, such as a down payment on a house, I recommend using a money market fund. Mutual funds and bank

CDs are other options for saving. I don't recommend withdrawing money from your Roth IRA for such uses. Remember, your goal is to save 10% for your financial independence. You can't spend the money and still expect to meet your goal.

If you are saving for a house down payment, use a money market fund or other savings instead of your Roth IRA.

If you know that you are likely to spend the money within five years, the best choices are CDs, money market funds, or some other safe, short-term investment. Use mutual funds or perhaps real estate if you know your holding time will exceed five years.

Avoid Annuities before 50

If you are under 50 years old, don't let a salesperson talk you into annuities. Annuities are somewhat similar to IRAs or 401(k) plans, in that you cannot touch the money until you are 59 1/2, unless you'd like to give Uncle Sam a 10% tax penalty, plus pay income taxes on all the growth on the money you withdraw.

Annuities are so often recommended because salespeople can make 6-8% first-year commissions from each sale. With $50,000 to invest, your annuity salesperson could earn an 8% commission, making $4,000 immediately, even if the person never lays eyes on you again or never offers advice in the future.

And guess what? If you decide a year or two later to cash out of the annuity, not only do you pay income tax and the 10% penalty, but you also pay a surrender charge that is essentially a back-end commission. The charges are similar to B share mutual funds—7-9% the first year, reducing 1% per year after that. So you are typically stuck in the annuity seven to nine years before you can get out without paying a surrender charge.

> **A salesperson can make 6% to 8% in the first-year commission when selling an annuity. If you decide to cash out of the annuity, you must pay taxes, penalties, *and* a back-end commission.**

If you are under 50 years old and a salesperson suggests that you roll over an IRA or a 401(k) plan into an annuity, run! You can be certain that the person is trying to make a quick commission without your best interest at heart. Rolling a retirement plan into an annuity is essentially putting a tax shelter inside a tax shelter. Fees and expenses will cost you more each year, and you will be stuck with the annuity for many years before you can get out without the surrender charge. Have a little fun: Look your salesperson in the eye and ask what benefit you receive from placing a tax shelter inside another tax shelter. You will probably find him or her stuttering and dancing around for a good answer.

While I highly discourage annuities for people under age 50, I can cite one notable exception. If you are a professional athlete or entertainer making megabucks in your 20s or 30s, an annuity might make sense for you. However, since such a profile represents such a tiny portion of the population, I won't go into detail here.

> **If you are under 50 years old, avoid investing in annuities.**

How to Choose a Financial Advisor

If I were a young investor, the first thing I would do is buy several good basic books on financial planning, and then I would learn how to become an effective investor. If you find your heartbeat quickening and a passion growing in you to learn to become a great investor as you read material about investing, you probably will accomplish just that in time. Keep reading, studying, and going to classes—and practice, practice, practice! Anyone who wants to become an accomplished investor can do so. It's easier today than ever before, thanks largely to the Internet.

However, if you are reading with a sinking heart and an emerging headache, all the while telling yourself that this is too hard, too boring, or too overwhelming, then you might be a perfect candidate for hiring professional financial help. A few pointers may help you select someone who can do a good job for you.

For starters, let's explain the terminology. You can hire a financial advisor, a financial consultant, a financial planner, an investment advisor, an investment consultant, a stockbroker, an insurance agent, or a CERTIFIED FINANCIAL PLANNER™. You can find excellent resources in any of the categories, and you can also find those who are downright terrible. The key is to recognize the difference as you interview prospects.

Start your interview process with an open mind. Walk in with the possibility that the person is terrific, but hold open the possibility that he or she is terrible. Plan to ask about an hour's worth of questions to secure a good feel for which category is most fitting. You may want to ask the following questions:

- *How long have you been in this business?*

It's important to know that 95% of all people who enter financial services leave the industry within five years.

- *Will you please describe the positions you have held in this business?*

Make the person give specific answers. Previous clerks, secretaries, and assistants may not possess enough knowledge to be useful to you.

- *How long have you been investing your own money?*

I personally would not hire someone who had been investing his or her own money for less than 10 years. You don't want someone to learn with your money.

- *How much of your own money do you save each year?*

I don't recommend working with someone who does not save at least 10% of his or her own income each year. You cannot teach what you do not know, and most knowledgeable people would agree that becoming financially independent requires saving 10% every year for about 30 years. By hiring someone who cares passionately about becoming rich someday, it is probable that that person is more likely to care about helping you do the same.

- *What is your educational background?*

Specifically ask about the person's business-related or investment/financial planning education.

- *How many hours of continuing education do you complete each year?*

The answer should be at least 15 per year; 25 or more is much better.

- *Why did you decide to get into this business?*

The people who tell you that they have been investors for many years and have always had a passion for investing generally will accomplish the best job for you. Many people go into the business because they hear about high income potential. Of course, no one will tell you that, but you'll need to read between the lines—i.e. what don't they say?

- *How are you paid?*

You will most often be better off if the fee is based upon an hourly rate or a fee of 1% or less of the investment assets under management.

- *Do you recommend specific stocks or mutual funds? If stocks, who chooses and monitors them?*
- *If mutual funds, do you recommend A shares, B shares, or C shares?*

You already know to run if the person wants to sell you A shares or B shares.

- *Do you recommend annuities for people like me?*

If you are under 50 and the person says *yes*, that's a big caution sign.

- *Are you a CERTIFIED FINANCIAL PLANNER™? If so, for how long? If not, why not?*

The CFP® designation is considered the gold standard in this business. Most people who stay in the industry for more than 5 years get a CFP® designation. A few exceptions exist, but not many.

- *Have any customers filed complaints against you? Have you ever been subject to censure or disciplinary action by security authorities? Do you have any "yes" answers on your U-4?*

The U-4 document reports on a financial advisor's history, and the form is on file with the government. Surprisingly, although I have been a CFP® practitioner since 1988, I have had only one prospective client ask me this question! Wow! Someone could possess a long history of taking advantage of clients, and you'd never know unless you asked!

- *Will you advise me on estate planning? Purchasing real estate and obtaining a mortgage? Tax planning? Employee benefits? Insurance? College fund planning? Retirement planning?*

Since you will be paying your advisor, you want to consider the scope of the advice he or she will be offering.

No matter who recommended a specific financial advisor to you, don't enter the office having decided to hire the person on someone's referral. Ask these questions and be comfortable with the answers before you make a decision to trust someone with your money.

Many people assume they must have a large sum of money saved up before they should hire a financial planner, but this isn't necessarily so. If you realize you could use some help, then whatever you spend on financial advice will likely become an excellent investment for you. A good financial planner can help you with every topic in this book, not just investments. Some will charge an hourly fee and forgo a minimum savings requirement.

A good financial planner can help you with every topic in this book.

Now, let's review the actions you will want to accomplish before investing:

- Use good asset allocation so that not more than 15% is in any one category.
- Diversify your investments by using mutual funds.
- Use index mutual funds if you are just starting to invest.
- Interview a financial advisor thoroughly before entrusting your money.

Action Step 11: First determine your risk tolerance, then choose an appropriate asset allocation, then select mutual funds to match this allocation plan.

Chapter 12

How Important Is Your Credit Score?

Get to know two things about a man: How he earns his money and how he spends it. You will then have the clue to his character. You will have a searchlight that reveals the inmost recesses of his soul. You know all you need to know about his standards, his motives, his driving desires, his real religion.

~ Robert J. McCracken

Components of Your Credit Score

Everyone who has ever borrowed money is likely to have a credit score with the credit bureaus. This score tells others how creditworthy you are. The criteria include: how much debt you have; your history for paying your debt on time; any adverse credit history you might have, such as bankruptcy or not paying some of your debts. Your score also factors in points for how long your credit has been established, how much

145

credit you have applied for recently, and how many different credit cards and other types of debt you have.

As you probably already know, a high credit score is important. When you borrow money, the interest rate on your debt will depend largely on your credit score. Someone with an excellent credit score (say, 760 or above) might acquire credit cards for 9% interest (or less), while someone with bad credit might have to pay perhaps 25%—that is, if he or she can get the credit card at all. Before you apply for your first mortgage, find out what your credit score is. If it's too low to qualify for the best interest rates, consider postponing buying the house until you can improve your credit score.

Your credit score will determine whether you will be able to obtain credit, as well as the interest rate you will pay.

Are you someone who has never used a credit card or never taken out a loan in your own name? If you are one of the few who has used only your debit card or cash for all purchases, you can be proud that you are completely debt free. The downside, however, is that you will also have no credit score. Since a credit bureau requires a *credit* history to create a credit report, gaining approval for a mortgage loan will be difficult without a credit history that shows you can be counted on to pay your bills.

If you never use credit, I recommend applying for a credit card immediately. Use it once a month and pay your balance in full every month. You will gradually build a credit history and gain a credit score, all without paying any interest charges.

You need to establish credit if you ever plan to obtain a mortgage to buy a house.

Credit Scores and Interest Rates

Credit scores fall within specific ranges, or bands, and a single lender generally extends everyone in a particular band the same interest rate on a loan. Still, you'll want to shop around when you plan to borrow money because different lenders will offer different rates for each band. For example, Lender A may offer loans at 7% for everyone in the top band, while Lender B will offer loans at 7.5% for everyone in the top band. Bands will typically fall in a chart like the one below:

Top score	760-850
Band 2	700-759
Band 3	660-699
Band 4	620-659
Band 5	580-619
Band 6	500-579
Worst score	300-499

However, the bands can differ from lender to lender. One lender's top band might be 770-850, while another classifies its top band as 750-850. We will come back to this point shortly to discuss how the classifications affect you.

FICO score

The most common term for your credit score is your FICO score. The name originates from Fair Isaac Corporation, which created the FICO score. The process involves an applied neural net technology (similar to artificial intelligence), a device most banks and telephone companies use to catch credit fraud and identity theft. We also have three main credit bureaus in this country, and each calls its credit score by a different name. For example, the Fast Start score is produced by Experian-Scorex, a competitor of Fair Isaac.

In early 2006, the three credit bureaus announced that they would together develop a single, unified credit-scoring model that all three would use to score borrowers in the exact same

147

way. Some believe the possibility is unlikely since FICO has a dominant market share of more than 90%.

The most important part of your credit score is based upon how consistently you pay your bills on time. In fact, this measure accounts for 35% of your total FICO score. If you pay all your bills on time consistently, you will earn the maximum possible score in this area.

By far, the most important part of your credit score is based on how consistently you pay your bills on time.

The second most important component is the total amount of debt you have outstanding. For example, you might have a mortgage, student loans, a car loan, plus credit cards. A portion of your score here will be based on the balances carried on your credit cards compared to your total credit limits on your cards.

Let's consider the following example: In one scenario, you have one credit card with a limit of $5,000 and $3,000 in charges. In another scenario, you instead have two credit cards, each with a $5,000 limit and $3,000 in outstanding debt split between the two cards. In the second case, you'll actually obtain a better score. Here's why:

$$\$3,000 \div \$10.000 = .30 \text{ or } 30\%$$
$$\$3,000 \div \$5,000 = .60 \text{ or } 60\%$$

A combined debt of $3000 divided by a combined credit line of $10,000 equals a lower ratio (30%) than a single debt of $3,000 divided by a credit line of $5,000 (60%). The magnitude of your debt ratio affects your FICO score. In general, the total borrowed on your credit cards should be 30% or less than the total credit limits available in order to earn a top score.

The example above highlights why you should not close many credit cards at the same time. Clearly, if you close out an account, the maximum of your total available credit decreases, so your balances appear larger as a *percentage* of your available credit.

That increase impacts your credit ratio unfavorably, and your FICO score may be hurt as a result. You should be aware that the primary situation in which your credit ratio can be a harmful factor is when you are applying for a new loan or mortgage. My advice is to pay off or pay down your credit cards before applying for a new loan, especially a mortgage. Then, once that loan is approved, consider closing all of the cards except two.

If you have multiple credit cards and decide to use only two, I recommend that you keep the cards you have had the longest for the benefit of the longest possible credit history. My advice assumes neither of the two cards you would keep has an annual fee. If a card carries an annual fee, close it and use a no-fee card.

If you are well-disciplined with your credit cards, paying them in full each month, then it is a good idea to accept a credit limit increase. Let's say that you have a $5,000 limit on one of your cards and you rarely charge more than $1,500 in a month, paying it in full when you receive each monthly statement. If the credit card company increases your limit to $8,000, simply keep spending below $1,500 in any given month—you will immediately improve your FICO score! (The ratio 1500/8000 is better than 1500/5000—do the math!)

In spite of everything we just covered, your credit score can suffer if your outstanding credit on your card is extremely high even if you pay your balances in full every month. I experienced this personally three years ago when my husband and I obtained a new mortgage. I had assumed that my score would be well into the 800 range. I was shocked and annoyed that it was only 790. Since I always paid my bills on time, paid all credit cards in full every month, and had no debt other than a *small* mortgage, I couldn't figure out why my score was below 800.

The problem was that we sometimes have relatively high balances (often a combined $20,000 in a month) on our credit cards. You see, we both travel extensively for business and charge much of our routine expenses for ease of record keeping. The credit bureaus have no way of measuring income or even knowing that we pay our cards in full every single month. They see only $20,000 in credit card balances, and we lose points, as these would be considered high balances for most.

A few years later, I obtained my credit score at a time when our credit card balances were extremely low. Sure enough, my score was well over 800. What's most important for you to remember is this: Pay down as much debt—particularly credit card debt—as you possibly can before you apply for a mortgage. It can make a significant difference in your credit score, which will translate into a major difference in the interest rate that you receive on the loan.

Keep Credit Card Balances Below 30%

As a reminder, the magic ratio of debt that you want on your credit cards is 30% or less. If you should close any credit cards, make sure that your typical outstanding debt will be less than 30% of the total credit lines available on the cards that remain open. Bear in mind that you'll earn a better credit score if your ratio is 20%—and an even better score if it's 10%.

Part of the second component of your credit score is the ratio of your outstanding debt to the total available debt. Keep your ratio under 30% at all times.

The length of your credit history determines the next portion of your credit score. If, for example, you acquired your first credit card three months ago and have no other credit history, you'll earn low points in this category. For this reason, I recommend to my clients that they obtain a joint credit card with their college-aged children. The action accomplishes two important objectives: First, it helps students establish four-year credit histories before they even graduate. Second, it helps parents monitor students' credit habits to teach their children about managing their credit and spending wisely.

The next component of your score is determined by the number of new accounts you have opened recently plus how many of your recent applications for credit have been reported.

Say someone buys a new house, a new car, opens two credit cards, and takes out a loan for appliances at about the same time. Such an individual will lose some points on his or her credit score. However, mortgage companies recognize that smart consumers shop for several mortgages before making a final decision. So within a brief window of time, you can apply for several mortgages simultaneously without adversely affecting your credit score.

The final factor in your credit score is relative to the variety in the types of credit you have carried. Overall, those who have had a mortgage, a car loan, a consumer loan, and credit cards will typically score higher than those who have had only a credit card or a student loan. Essentially, credit bureaus examine how well you can handle different types of debt. The more variety in your credit history, the higher your score will be.

One important caveat must be added here: You will be awarded a better score with outstanding balances on one or two credit cards than you would if you had balances on seven or eight cards, even if the total dollar amount outstanding is identical!

The last three components making up your credit score are the length of your credit history, the number of new accounts opened lately, and the variation in the types of debt you have had.

The following is a breakdown of how each component affects your FICO score:

How well you pay your bills on time	35%
Total debt outstanding	30%
How long your credit history has been established	15%
How many new accounts or credit applications you have	10%
The variation in the types of debt you have had	10%

As you can see, paying your bills on time and not having excessive debt are the most critical components. If you have a credit card with a $5,000 limit and a balance of $4,998, your credit score will suffer. Alternatively, a credit card with a limit of $10,000 and a balance of about $3,000 or less will result in a higher credit score. I can't stress enough that lenders like to see a ratio of 30% or less.

Take a moment to refer back to the chart that shows the various bands in the credit-scoring system. Typically, the top scores fall within the band of 760-850. Now, you might recall the situation I mentioned in which I was frustrated with my FICO score of 790. At that time, however, I still received the same interest rate as if my score were 850. Let's now also consider the opposite scenario—falling within the high end of a lower band. If your score is 755 when you are preparing to buy a house, you should take immediate action to raise your score to 760. Moving up to a higher band will lower the interest rate you are offered on your mortgage. Ultimately, learn from different lenders what the minimum credit score would be for you to fall within their highest band. Particularly relative to a mortgage, the cutoff —whether it is 740, 750, 760 or 770—can vary among lenders. Most certainly, you should ask.

If you want more information about your credit report or your FICO score, go to www.myFICO.com. As you will see on this website, the US population's scores break down in the following manner:

Score	% of the population
800+	13%
750-799	27%
700-749	18%
650-699	15%
600-649	12%
550-599	8%
500-549	5%
<499	2%

Why Do Lenders Use Credit Scores?

The answer is simple: The scores are historically proven to be extremely reliable. People exhibit certain credit habits that tend to be consistent. For example, those with high scores typically pay their bills on time, keep low credit balances, and don't use a great deal of consumer debt. Consequently, as individuals who are likely to apply for credit that they will repay, they are good credit risks.

At the other end of the spectrum are those who have debt up to their ears with credit cards all maxed out and who consistently spend more than they earn. They are often late with payments and are forever trying to get new debt to pay off old debt, or to buy yet another toy that they cannot afford. A situation like that is a bankruptcy waiting to happen, and the lenders know this. Thus, such individuals receive low credit scores, and the lenders who deal with them can charge extremely high interest rates.

> **Lenders rely on credit scores because the ratings have proven extremely reliable.**

Free Credit Report Every Year

The good news is that everyone can obtain a free credit report once a year from each of the three credit reporting agencies:

Equifax:	www.equifax.com
Experian:	www.experian.com
TransUnion:	www.transunion.com

Your credit report will not include your FICO score; however, the score is available for a small fee.

Huge caution: If you want your credit report or FICO score, *never* type "free credit report" into your Web browser in search of one on the Internet. Dozens of scam artists are ready to steal your identity easily if you have the misfortune of visiting that sort of website.

Also, going directly to the credit bureaus' websites in order to obtain your free credit report poses some challenges. They all want to sell you something. I've invested some sleuthing time to find the link that delivers a truly free credit report without strings attached to some package deal. With that, I recommend visiting this website: www.annualcreditreport.com. There you can acquire a free credit report from each of the three bureaus simultaneously. Better yet, consider staggering your requests and ask for one report every four months.

> **Everyone is entitled to a free credit report every year from each of the three credit reporting agencies.**

If you want your FICO score, you have to buy it from one of only two places that sell it: www.myFICO.com and www.Equifax.com. I don't recommend that you buy a credit score from Experian or TransUnion, as lenders rarely use their proprietary scores.

You'll notice that all three credit-reporting companies and Fair Isaac offer annual services that you can buy to monitor your credit reports. (Be forewarned that the monitoring service does not prevent identity theft; it only provides monthly alerts that can help you deal with the problem sooner than you might otherwise.) I started using one recently because I decided that if I ever become a victim of identity theft, I want to reduce the hassle of straightening out all the issues. I'd rather fork over $5 per month than deal with a tremendous problem. If this type of surveillance appeals to you, consider checking with your insurance agent. They will sometimes sell such a service to you for approximately $15 a year.

> **Paying for a monitoring service with a credit bureau will not prevent identity theft, but it will notify you about it so you can act quickly.**

What about Errors?

If you notice an error on your credit report, click on the link indicated on the credit bureau's website to report it. If the issue appears to be serious, such as someone having taken out a credit card in your name, you are likely a victim of identity theft. Taking action immediately is imperative. Report the theft to all three reporting agencies and have them flag your account with a fraud alert. As soon as possible, you will also need to take the steps necessary to remove the erroneous information from your credit bureau report while closing the account that was used fraudulently. Additionally, you will want to file a local police report as well as a report with the Federal Trade Commission (FTC), the federal agency tasked with dealing with identity theft: http://www.consumer.gov/idtheft/.

If someone has stolen your identity, report the theft to the three credit bureaus and to the FTC immediately, as well as file a local police report. Take action at once to correct your credit bureau report.

I once sold a townhouse to a woman in a transaction that called for her to assume my first mortgage. Somehow, when she went bankrupt five years later, her bankruptcy showed up on my credit bureau report, even though the mortgage was no longer in my name. The mistake was clear, but I still spent many hours talking on the phone and writing letters to straighten out the error. If I had not bothered to correct the misinformation, my credit score would have suffered significantly.

Be sure to obtain your credit report at least once each year and, again, review it carefully, checking for any errors. Give such an annual credit report review the same priority as you would your annual dental exam. While you don't anticipate any cavities, an appointment with your dentist confirms what you need to know! Similarly, make a point each year to confirm that all your records are correct; be certain that no one has tried to steal your identity.

Check Your FICO Score

Whenever you are planning to apply for any major debt, such as a mortgage or car loan, make a wise investment, which is well worth the money, to obtain your FICO score. Then, as we discussed earlier, if you find that your score is near the next highest band, take immediate action to improve your score before applying for credit. After you implement the necessary changes, you'll need to wait an additional thirty days or so, as your score won't improve until the changes are reported to the credit bureaus.

If your score is lower than you want it to be, two possible "quick fixes" are available: One is to pay down your debt, particularly your credit cards. This action will make more of a difference than any other single thing you can do. The other is immediately to correct any errors reported on your file. Most errors affect scores negatively, and removing negative information will, of course, improve your score.

Other Uses of Credit History

You should know how critical your credit history is for factors other than obtaining credit. For example, many employers run credit reports on potential employees. If the report is terrible, a job offer may not be extended; many employers believe that people who can't handle their money well are, in general, irresponsible.

> **Among other factors, your credit history might impact your ability to obtain a good job offer.**

Additionally, insurance companies often run credit-based scores before deciding to issue an insurance policy. If you have a low score, they may determine that you are overly likely to file a claim and, therefore, seem a bad risk for them. They may refuse to issue insurance to you.

Landlords will usually run credit scores. They know that if a potential tenant has a poor score, he or she is more likely to have trouble paying the rent.

Cell phone companies also run credit scores, as you may already know. They will not sign a contract with you if your credit score is too weak.

Ultimately, your credit score tells the world whether or not you are responsible. If your score falls at 700 and above, pat yourself on the back. If you maintain a high credit score, your interest rates on any debt will be as low as possible, and your road to becoming rich will be far easier!

Action Step 12: Earn a credit score of 700 or higher, and keep it there.

Chapter 13
Getting Rich More Quickly

Man is a goal-seeking animal. His life only has meaning if he is reaching out and striving for his goals.

> ~ Aristotle

I f you have come this far, you are committed to handling your money well with the goal of becoming rich. You've learned that growing rich is easy, although usually accomplished over many years. By remaining free of debt and saving 10% of your income for 30 or 40 years, you'll wake up one day with the realization that you are, in fact, wealthy!

But who wants to get rich slowly? Isn't it more fun to get rich more quickly? If that's your attitude, then this chapter is for you.

A caveat: Avoid get-rich-quick schemes. They don't work. The way to get rich more quickly is to have the right attitude, keeping your mind focused on what you want and disregarding what you don't want. You also need to set attainable goals that you strive constantly to achieve, increasing them at regular intervals.

Be forewarned that what is about to follow is not what you would typically expect to hear from an older, established CERTIFIED FINANCIAL PLANNER™ practitioner. But I've included this chapter because I've personally experienced success in everything I'm sharing and I've seen it work with clients and friends. I know this approach works.

Attitude Is Most Important

From the beginning I've underscored the crucial need to understand that your beliefs about money will influence your ability to become wealthy more than any action you take or any investing technique you will ever learn. Put simply, people who expect to get rich do so; those with a poverty mentality remain poor. Even those who inherit or win the lottery end up poor again if they possess a poverty mentality. (Statistics show that the ones with the wrong mindset blow through that kind of money in fewer than seven years.)

The way you think and feel about money has more influence on wealth than anything.

Feeling angry, unhappy, or victimized are all negative emotions. Most certainly, when you feel negative, you attract a proportionate share of negativity into your life. Do you ever wake up on the wrong side of the bed and then spend the rest of the day on a downhill trend? That's my point! If you tell yourself that the day will be bad, invariably you will create a day you would not want to repeat.

While in my 20s, I applied this principle totally by accident. The accident was the fact that I held positive views about money. When I was 23, utterly broke, and using every cent that I possibly could to pay off my college debt, I never told myself how broke I was. Instead, I told myself how excited I was that I would be completely free of debt in 16 months, 11 months, and 4 months until...*boom*...my debt was gone!

160

When I first learned that I simply needed to save 10% of my income for 30 or 40 years to become wealthy, I remember my attitude: Wow, that's so easy! I can do that! I never thought the process would be hard. As a result, becoming rich has been an easy task for me! No matter how much I have earned, I have always saved at least 10%. I have always used a spending plan because I knew that putting aside money both for savings and for pleasure—clothes, travel, and entertainment—was necessary.

Thoughts and What You Create

To apply the principle, let's take a moment to understand its fundamental process: We create what we think about and what we feel. The principle has a mystical ring, and it does indeed work like magic. Those familiar with the concept often refer to it as the "Law of Attraction." Your thoughts attract everything that is in your life. Positive thoughts attract positive people, places, and things into your life. The reverse is equally true. The process can occur intentionally or by accident. (Not surprisingly, most of us create our realities by accident!)

Let's bring this back to the issue of money. If you tell yourself that saving is impossible and that you can never stretch your paycheck far enough, what do you think will occur? For certain, you will never manage to save money. Saying over and over that managing money is incredibly hard and all too confusing ensures that you will face an uphill climb.

Because they believe they never will have magnificent possessions and experiences, many quit dreaming about the wonders they would like to bring into their lives. When all they desire seems totally out of reach, frustration and unhappiness replace the dreams.

I challenge you to think differently. In this chicken and egg situation, I can tell you which one comes first: Thoughts come first! Your reality then follows from your thoughts. Therefore, if you are not particularly happy with your current reality, you can bank on the fact that your past thoughts helped create where you are today.

161

The million-dollar question is this: How do you change your thinking in order to attract abundance and all your heart's desires into your life? The first step is simply to become aware. Each time you catch yourself thinking negatively or in a limiting manner about money, make a point of noting the slip-up: "I just noticed that I was thinking I'm broke and can't afford that." No matter the specifics, begin by becoming aware.

> **The first step in changing your thinking is simply becoming aware.**

Your instruction here is to observe. Avoid judgment and condemnation; don't tell yourself that your thought is wrong. Take notice. If you can, laugh! Laughter releases negative thoughts and allows you to replace them more quickly with positive ones.

For example, assume you were thinking how you must live from paycheck to paycheck. You can say, "I noticed I said I struggle on the income I earn. I don't want to live paycheck to paycheck. I no longer want to create that reality in my life." The next step is to choose a deliberate thought that presents the way you want to live. You could tell yourself that many people in your circumstance successfully save money from every paycheck. Simply say, "I'm learning how to save as well. Every month, saving becomes easier. In no time at all, I'll be saving plenty of money."

When I am about to embark upon a new undertaking, one of my all-time favorite mind games is to tell myself that I'm super smart. If others can learn to do the task, then so can I. I remind myself that all tasks can be learned. From the day we were born, we began learning!

Start with Small Goals

In my experience, when telling myself I can do something, setting goals that allow baby steps works best. In the above example, for instance, if I said to myself that I could save money, I would consider a proportion that my brain would accept. Rather than choosing 25%, I would pick a smaller percentage as a goal. I need to tell myself what I deem to be reasonable goals so I will take the actions that enable me to achieve them.

You can perform specific exercises to expand your capacity to think positively and, likewise, to begin the process of creating highly positive energy about money. As your thoughts become more positive, you will attract a correlating increase in positive occurrences.

Chapter Two introduced the exercise of "spending" money daily on anything you desire. Truthfully, this is one of my favorite exercises, which I carry out by making my lists of expenditures in a daily journal. (A simple spiral notebook will suffice.)

If you recall, the exercise stipulates that you spend $1,000 of imaginary money on the first day. Your whim decides how to spend every penny. The only rule is that you can't save the money—you must spend it, whether on yourself, your family, your friends, your church, a favorite charity, or whatever you dream up.

Each day, increase the amount that you "spend" by $1,000. On day 10, your allowance is $10,000, and you will spend $58,000 on day 58. At the end of one year, you will spend $365,000 on the final day. If you add up your spending for the full 365 days, your total will exceed $66 million. The point is to begin expanding your thinking for the incredible reason that your mind can't distinguish between emotions that come from real experience versus emotions that stem from something imagined. Mind over matter is what makes this process powerful.

Let's play with a specific example. On the 90th day you allocate your $90,000 to splurge on $10,000 worth of beautiful new clothes. You send $20,000 to your parents for the vacation of a lifetime. You send another $25,000 to your favorite teacher from ninth grade along with a note about how she inspired you when you were in her class. You then spend $5,000 on magnificent front-row tickets to the big game, inviting your four best friends to join you. You also spend another $5,000 for a limo, an incredible dinner, and night on the town after the game.

Is that unbelievable? So far, you would have spent *only* $65,000. You still have $25,000 to go, just for today. So suppose you decide to donate the remaining cash to your favorite orphanage in Africa to lessen the suffering of children with AIDs. You can then go to bed knowing you can afford to be so generous because tomorrow you will have $91,000 more to spend, and the day after, you will have $92,000!

I felt incredible as I did this. My state of mind was as if I truly spent the money. I could feel the positive energy just bursting from me. I also found that the process allowed me to dream *big* in a way that I never had before. Once I *had* this money to spend, I started decorating to the hilt, making my yard extraordinarily beautiful, and buying clothes that would make the wealthiest Hollywood stars quite jealous. And let me tell you, the charities in town thought I was the greatest! My daily pleasure was immense despite the fact that every transaction occurred on paper.

Start with small, attainable goals and build upon them.

Visualizations

I am crazy about red. I would wear red suits every single day, if only I could find them. For some reason, red suits are scarce, so I own three—not thirty! Consequently, as I spent my imaginary money, I decided one day to buy a custom-made red suit with my play money. I got such a kick out of the purchase that I had two more suits made the next week, and three more tailored a few weeks later. At that rate, I was building an entire wardrobe of red suits, something I had always wanted.

Not long after, I was thinking about those red suits all the time. Within a few weeks, I decided to use them as a reward system for myself. I determined that the day I achieved a certain goal, I would reward myself with a real custom-made red suit. When I hit a second specific goal, I would reward myself with two custom-made suits. Then, when a third major goal was achieved, I intended to splurge on three more.

I took my red suits a further step. I began to visualize myself sitting on the couch next to Oprah Winfrey, discussing this book with her while wearing one of my beautiful custom-made red suits. I imagined the conversation she and I would have about this book. I rehearsed the dialogue in my head endlessly. I'm still writing the book, so the outcome is yet to be!

What is also important is the fact that the scenario makes sense to me. It is within my reach. Oprah has the biggest heart of anyone I have ever known. She is all about making this world a better place for as many people as she possibly can. She is extremely savvy and certainly aware of how many marriages break up over money issues. She knows that people live with fear and anxiety over money. Because this book encourages you to release your fears and to begin taking easy steps toward gaining financial independence, I know that Oprah would love to help share this message.

Even if spending imaginary money seems too odd or mystical, I challenge you to play the game. Stick to it for 90 days, if not the entire year. Skeptical minds tend to give up within 30 days. "It's ridiculous!" they say. I personally didn't begin to see a big difference in my own life until about day 50. I can still remember telling my personal coach, Joseph Dixon, about my turning point in one of my weekly sessions. I was grinning from ear to ear as I told him about the luxuries I had "bought" that day, and about the incredible charitable donations I had made. Not coincidentally, I was having an incredible month at work, attracting many great new clients, and making double the money I had made in the same month the previous year.

What you visualize with emotion will turn into reality.

Give Some Away

I adore the Murphy family, located here in the Atlanta area. John and Jeannette are parents to 26 children—3 biological and 23 adopted. The adopted children all have medical disabilities. Many have Down syndrome, some have heart problems, and one child is blind. I have been donating small amounts to them every month for several years, but I dream of the day when I can give them a significant sum of money. On several days during my spending exercise, I donated $20,000 to a new house fund for them. When the house was built, I began donating money for new appliances and new vans for the family. With their current needs met, I began donating money to fund a retirement plan for John and Jeannette. The feeling was exquisite!

From that exercise, I am determined to make everything I envisioned a reality someday. I don't know how and I don't know when, but I know that someday I will create far more money than I can ever spend, and I will gain the joy of making a significant contribution to the Murphys. In my mind I made it happen, so I know in advance that all the wonderful positive vibrations I'm sending out into the universe will attract what I need to create this reality one day. Stay tuned in a future book—and on *Oprah*—to hear about this happening!

> **Sending positive vibrations into the universe about helping others can make the vision a reality one day.**

Are you telling yourself that this is all too far out to happen? Then I will ask you a question: What do you have to lose by playing along? Five minutes each day isn't much time to play. And, meanwhile, what if I am right? What if you actually can create and attract abundance along with anything else you want in life by thinking about it? You might as well give the possibility a shot. Imagine how your life could be if by generating incredibly positive feelings about money enabled you to attract money into your life. Imagine a reality composed of all your desires!

Of course I'm not saying to spend all your time imagining and never take any action. Certainly, you have to take action, too! But most people will never take any action because their thoughts are so negative. You, however, will find that changing your thoughts will propel you into taking real action.

Mental Muscles

I'll mention again a book that I have used as a guide in teaching such principles: *Ask and It Is Given,* by Esther and Jerry Hicks. I have found tremendous merit in sharing such exercises that expand our ability to think and feel positively, and to attract what we desire. Establishing the right mental process is very important to creating wealth and abundance.

Another book that I bring up once more is *The Wealthy Spirit,* by Chellie Campbell. I so highly recommend this title that I buy a hundred copies at a time to give as gifts to clients and to my seminar attendees. The author provides one story to be read each day of the year, each one moving you gently toward your financial goals. The affirmations never fail to make me giggle and feel terrific. In turn, all those terrific feelings attract wonderful circumstances into my life.

Additionally, I especially appreciate Lynn Grabhorn's *Excuse Me, Your Life is Waiting,* which further explains how to use the principle of thinking positive thoughts and creating positive feelings in order to attract good into your life. Money is only one element. Every area of your life benefits—from wonderful relationships, excellent health, tremendous pleasure, great adventure, to whatever floats your boat!

Top athletes consistently apply this strategy. A basketball player will sit in a quiet room with eyes closed to imagine an outstanding performance on the court. The careful visualization of shots clearing the basket; thus, the anticipation of winning starts before the game and continues throughout play. Anyone who plays sports knows that the mind game must be won in order to play a winning game. Both positive and negative feelings play a role in the outcome.

How much time do you spend worrying and fretting about money? Transmitting negative energy results in financial difficulties. Do you notice such effects in your life? If so, what do you have to lose by trying something new? Or, in other words, imagine all that you have to gain by changing the tune you play in your head. Thinking about finances on a positive note has worked for countless people through the ages. For all the same reasons, the theory can work for you as well.

> **If you spend time worrying and fretting over money, the negative energy transmitted will return to you in financial difficulties.**

One of my favorite Bible verses seems appropriate here: "For as he thinks in his heart, so is he." (Proverbs 23:7.) No matter your faith, you can see that my message is certainly not new. Philosophers and scientists have understood the principle for thousands of years, and hundreds of generations of wise men and women have been putting their thoughts to work for them.

You know the old saying: *If you think you can, you can. If you think you can't, you can't.* Life truly is a self-fulfilling prophecy. Isn't it terrific that you can write your own script! You get to decide which prophecies you will create in your own life.

> **Life truly is a self-fulfilling prophecy. What is so terrific is that you can start writing your own script!**

Begin the practice of conscious thought today. No matter your expectations, you will be astonished by changes that appear in your life! If you are ready for the next step, consider buying other training materials from Brian Tracy, Zig Ziglar, Tony Robbins, Denis Waitley or Jim Rohn. Each can give you a wealth of step-by-step information to begin creating exactly the life you want. Also, *The Secret*, a DVD which does a fabulous job of explaining the "Law of Attraction," is currently available at www.thesecret.tv or in many bookstores, including www.amazon.com.

Use Goals

I bought Brian Tracy's *Psychology of Achievement* more than 20 years ago. I still listen to the recordings, repeatedly marveling at how I continue to learn more each time. This training has made a huge impact on my life in highlighting the critical need for clear, specific, measurable, written goals. Although I always had goals rattling around in my head, as well as endless "to do" lists, I didn't begin systematically to write my goals until I listened to Mr. Tracy's words. What a jet propulsion mechanism that was!

Studies have shown that one of the differences between highly successful people and those who are average is in the long-term approach of the successful. Long-term thinking motivates us to remain in school to earn advanced degrees. Long-term thinking inspires us to turn off the TV in order to spend time in making our relationships with our mate or our children strong. Long-term planning encourages us to exercise regularly and maintain a healthy weight. Clear, specific written goals are the best way that I know of to ensure that we stay focused on the long-term thinking rather than on whatever brings immediate pleasure or relief.

Although this is a book about money, I urge you to set goals for all areas of your life. Think about it: Each aspect of your life interacts with one another synergistically. When one goes well, the others typically do, too. When three are going well, the fourth and fifth are usually a snap. Conversely, when you are truly struggling in one area, other areas seem to be falling apart, too.

> **Because all the different areas of your life interact with one another synergistically, it's important to set goals for each aspect of your life.**

If one of your goals is to have a happy, healthy marriage, managing your money well can make a huge difference. The result will be fewer fights over money; hence, a more harmonious marriage follows.

If your goal is to enjoy excellent health and fitness, the choice will impact your financial future as well. Compare the medical expenses of a slim individual with low cholesterol versus one who is one hundred pounds overweight with diabetes and high blood pressure. What a huge financial impact your health decisions can have!

The categories that I use for my goals include the following:

- Faith – all of my spiritual goals.

- Family – my goals for the relationships I want with my wonderful husband, my two incredible sons, my very special sister, and my extended family.

- Friends – my goals for the kinds of friendships I want to have and the time and commitment I will make to my special friends.

- Fitness – my health, nutrition, weight, and exercise goals.

- Finances (job related) – the goals I want to achieve in my business.

- Finances (personal) – my savings and investment goals.

- Fun – my goals for such activities as playing bridge, riding my bicycle, tap dancing, traveling and watching movies.

- Finishing touches – my personal growth and education goals.

- For others – my service and charitable giving goals.

I write specific goals for each category, updating them every year and always keeping a copy of the old ones. I can't tell you how thrilling it is to look at the goals I wrote in 1986 and see how they have all been accomplished. The more I see those results, the more courage and confidence I have in setting bigger and bigger goals.

Now, for example, one of my top goals is to complete this book and have it published. Afterwards, my goal is to discuss the book with Oprah on her television show, thereby exposing my message to more people more quickly, ultimately changing their lives by providing the tools needed for financial independence. I want to be the "Money Mom" for millions of young people, making a difference in their lives as my mother did in mine.

Moving Quickly

Once you have written out your goals, certain methods will help you turbo charge your goals so that they are easier and quicker to achieve. I have a host of techniques that I use which are so powerful that they continue to blow me away.

- Quickly write out your top goals first thing each day, summarizing each with a word or two. Every morning I use a notepad in the bathroom while brushing my teeth. Because I have quick abbreviations for each key goal, I finish writing in less than a minute—well before I finish brushing!

- Meditate each day about your goals. Visualize yourself living the achievement of your goals. Every day I envision myself discussing my book with Oprah.

- Tell all of your supportive friends and family members about your goals so they can be your cheerleaders. Don't share your goals with any naysayer—you don't need the negative energy!

171

- Pray every day. Ask God or the higher power you believe in to show you what to do next in order to move you toward your goals. You will be amazed by how effectively prayer sets your radar antennae in your brain. You'll begin noticing situations and encountering people which are exactly what you need to advance your goals.

- Read something every day that will move you toward one or more of your goals. Your mind needs rich mental protein to be growing all the time. After I pray, meditate, and journal during my morning routine, I always spend at least 15 minutes reading a book to help me improve the book I am writing.

- When you enter your office or workplace, write down the top five tasks that you will accomplish that day, in order from most to least important, before you begin any activity. Resolve that you will not finish your workday until at least the top three are finished. Keep your mind on that list all day, and do not let trivial matters that arise during the day throw you off track.

- Make an effort to join a high-achievers' mastermind group. I am in a CEO Roundtable group, which is offered by my local NAWBO (National Association of Women Business Owners) chapter. I meet monthly for two and a half hours with 10 other high-achieving women, and we share our goals, exchange good ideas, and cheer one another on. The icing on the cake is that we have become wonderful friends as well!

- Spend some time every day listening to books on tape or

to recordings about any subject that will fast-forward your actions toward your goals. I use car driving time and the time getting dressed in the morning for my listening.

- Start a journal, jotting down the little events that happen each day, situations that seem to be moving you toward your goals. I journal at least one page per day. Currently, I begin my journal page each day by "spending" my $1,000s per day, increasing my play money by $1,000 each day. After several lines that describe how I am spending today's money, I quickly write out abbreviated reminders of my top goals. *CR 2 wk* stands for my goal of visiting my son Blake for two weeks in Costa Rica, where he is studying.

My next step is to write down all the synchronicities I've noticed in the last 24 hours, as well as any answers to prayer or movement toward my goals. For example, I attended a lunch meeting with about 60 businesswomen, and one of the women I met teaches tap dance for adults. I've wanted to learn to tap dance for 50 years! I met another woman who has a client who is a publicist specializing in book authors. This woman also helps authors sell products related to their books, such as workbooks, tapes, CDs, and seminars. With all three of those goals written in my journal, I was attracting people into my life to help me achieve them.

- Finally, express gratitude. I finish my journal page with gratitude for all the good that happened to me in the last 24 hours. If you want more of something, then express appreciation for what you already have. From there, watch the good things grow. (If you gripe about something, you can watch your bellyaches grow, too!)

I could extend this list to include many more items, but those mentioned are what I believe most effectively turbo charge my life. I perform most tasks virtually every day, and I attend the mastermind group every month without fail. I find that the hour I invest every morning in my quiet time makes my whole day incredible and rich with opportunities and answered prayers. If I happen to skip that quiet time, rushing out of the house on rare days, nothing seems to get finished quickly or efficiently, and much of the day is wasted. When I take the time each morning to focus on what I plan to accomplish, I often astonish myself with how much I achieve in a day.

Find a way to turbo charge your goals.

If you build the habit of incorporating these actions into your everyday life, you will become noticeably more valuable to your employer. As a valuable employee, you will earn larger raises and faster promotions. As a business owner who operates this way, you will find business growing faster with less effort!

I recently met a woman who had divorced a few years prior. She had left the marriage with $40,000 in debt and no investments or savings. She was determined to free herself of debt and become a millionaire. Less than five years after divorcing, she has no debt, she has saved $50,000, and she believes she will hit her millionaire goal in less than 10 years. She invested in a Zig Ziglar (who is a fabulous motivational speaker) seminar and began to change her thinking, which allowed her to raise her income over 50%. How did she save so much so quickly? Upon determining that she could maintain her spending at her current level, she began to place all additional income straight into savings after she'd paid her taxes and satisfied her objective for charitable giving.

Her goal today is to increase her earnings by at least 50% again in the next two years. I have no doubt she will achieve her objective, as she is taking action to accomplish a clear, specific goal that she keeps in mind constantly.

Again and again, I have witnessed that when people decide to become millionaires with a true commitment to making it happen, they generally do so in 10 to 20 years. I believe *anyone* can become a millionaire in 30 to 40 years if one simply remains free of debt and saves at least 10% each year, investing intelligently. The process doesn't take much thought or effort.

On the other hand, if you are one who wants to make the goal happen faster, you can do so with some extra thought and effort. When you begin to focus like a laser beam, you will find yourself doing whatever it takes. As in the example of the woman who was divorced and greatly in debt, she put her mind and her actions to work.

Others who are determined to become rich quickly find ways to cut their spending, as we have discussed previously. You might be astonished to learn how many people, focused on being wealthy, find ways to save 20% or 30% or even 50% of their income!

Expect Seasons

My husband and I find that the money we are able to save varies with the season of our lives. In certain seasons we save only 10% because we're spending money on other important areas, such as our kids' college educations. In other seasons, we can minimize our spending and save 30% or more.

Looking back over the years, I found I had a season of high savings before my kids were born. While paying for daycare, I saved less and the percentage declined. My savings increased again during their school years, and then fell with the arrival of their college days and tuition bills. Now that they are grown, the savings have increased again. Remain positive throughout your slow savings periods, reminding yourself that you possess the discipline to say no to the budget busters.

Always bear in mind that lower savings periods are usually temporary. Don't get discouraged if your saving slows considerably. Remember that you will later return to putting aside the maximum amount of money possible for your financial independence.

Savings will vary from season to season.

Again, it all comes down to attitude. People who are determined to get rich more quickly (not with schemes, but with the old-fashioned method of saving and staying out of debt) gain an almost magical power to make it happen. They find opportunities to make more money. New job offers at higher salaries seem to find them. Opportunities for outside income abound.

One of my favorite popular sayings is that winners do what losers don't like to do. So if the list above seems a bit overwhelming, gently talk yourself into believing you can accomplish whatever you set out to achieve. We all start at the beginning, and we all learn along the way. When I initiated my morning discipline, I kept telling myself that I was a winner, and that I was willing to pay the price that winners pay to create fabulous lives. Admittedly, in the beginning, I did not love my morning quiet time. With persistence, however, I gradually started to enjoy my hour to reflect, plan and express gratitude. Today, I would not want to start my day any other way.

Winners do what losers don't like to do.

Make it happen. You wouldn't have read to this far if you weren't a winner!

Action Step 13: Decide to follow what top achievers do in order to turbo charge the achievement of your goals.

Chapter 14

Why the Rich Sleep Soundly at Night

To be happy means to be free, not from pain or fear, but from care or anxiety.

~ W.H. Auden

In this final chapter, we will cover a few other matters worth your attention so that your financial house can stand in order—and so you can sleep soundly without worries. In the interest of brevity, we'll touch on each topic with enough information for you to take the first wise steps. These subjects will be discussed in detail in a later book.

Preparing for the Dastardly Ds

No one is immune to the "dastardly Ds": death, disability, disease, disaster, dents, dementia, and destruction. If you possess objects of value, you need to insure them.

177

Car Insurance

You need car insurance, and the trick is to obtain the necessary amount of coverage without overspending. Consider several ideas: Use a $1,000-collision deductible if you possibly can. Or drop the collision coverage completely if you are driving an old clunker, particularly if you are young. Make sure that you carry at least $300,000 of liability insurance under your automobile policy.

Renter's or Homeowner's Insurance

You need either renter's or homeowner's insurance. If you are renting an apartment or a house, the contents—clothing, furniture and computer—will be covered from loss from a fire or a robbery *only if* you have renter's insurance. I suggest the following rule of thumb in determining whether to buy such protection: If you can afford to replace all of your furniture, clothes and electronic equipment without any problem, you do not need renter's insurance. However, if replenishing everything would be a hardship, purchase the insurance.

When you buy a house, you must carry homeowner's insurance or the mortgage company will not approve your loan. If you own jewelry, silver, furs, collectibles, antiques or other valuables worth more than $1,000, you need to acquire a personal articles floater to cover these pieces individually. Be sure that you also protect yourself with $300,000 of liability coverage on your homeowner's policy.

Medical Insurance

Everyone needs medical insurance! Even if you are young and healthy, you should purchase some basic coverage from a private policy if you are not covered by any insurance through your job. To make such insurance affordable, choose a high deductible such as $2,000 or $5,000. If you absolutely cannot afford any policy, talk to your parents. Many are willing to buy medical insurance for their young adult children.

Life Insurance

I have to be blunt when I ask: Will someone suffer from not having your income if you should die? You do not need life insurance if no one is dependent on you for an income. However, if you have children or a baby on the way, carrying life insurance is imperative. Except under special circumstances, I recommend purchasing inexpensive term insurance. You can research options on the Internet or talk with an insurance agent.

Disability Insurance

If you are young, your most valuable asset is most likely your ability to earn a living. Therefore, the most important insurance is disability insurance. Such a policy provides a payment to you each month in the event that you become sick or otherwise disabled and unable to work. If your employer offers disability insurance, jump on the opportunity to buy as much coverage as you possibly can. If you are self-employed and have to buy your own coverage, you will find this type of insurance to be expensive. Nevertheless, buy a policy the moment you can possibly afford it.

Long-Term Care Insurance

The ideal time to buy long-term care insurance is when you are around 50, and preferably no later than age 60. If your parents are in the 50 to 70 age range, certainly talk to them to ensure they own this coverage. Why? If something happens to your parents and they cannot afford their own long-term care expenses, the burden will probably fall upon you.

Umbrella Liability Insurance

Umbrella liability insurance is essentially lawsuit insurance. It protects you if someone who is hurt at your home or by your car decides to sue you. Generally coverage starts at $1 million, but the policies are inexpensive. Typically, $1 million of coverage will cost $15 to $20 a month. I would recommend that you hold umbrella liability insurance if you own an expensive house or car, or if you earn a six-figure income. Talk to the insurance agent from whom you buy your auto insurance and/or homeowner's insurance about purchasing the umbrella liability insurance.

Taxes

The most crucial tax point to remember: Never mess with the IRS. You must file a tax return every year whether you like it or not. Filing for taxes is easy nowadays with all the terrific computer software available. I particularly recommend TurboTax, Tax Cut or Tax Act. The software should cost you about $20 to $30 per year.

Tax software prompts you to respond to questions so that you can determine whether you should either itemize your deductions or use a standard deduction. Choose the route the software recommends. Make sure you file electronically, particularly if you anticipate a refund.

Consider using Quicken or Microsoft Money to track your finances during the year, as this will make preparing taxes much easier. The time to start looking for a good accountant is when your adjusted gross income exceeds $150,000.

All in all, rather than grumbling about taxes, be grateful that you live in the land of opportunity! No one in any other country in the world faces the many options that we have as Americans to make money. A little gratitude for that will make the tax process far less painful.

Legal Topics

Everyone needs a will, which is a document that states to whom your belongings go in the event that you die. If you are quite young and own little property of value, you can simply write a handwritten will. Have someone witness your signature.

Once you begin to accumulate more property, consider purchasing one of the will preparation software packages available for about $25.

Once you have children or a baby on the way, a well written will is imperative. You will particularly want to plan for the possibility of both parents dying at the same time. Naming a guardian for your children, as well as a trustee who will manage any money left to raise them, is important. Such planning is especially imperative if you have life insurance because the amount of money to manage will be significant. If you have a child, I strongly recommend that you hire an attorney to prepare your will rather than drafting it yourself.

> **Once you have a baby on the way, a will is imperative. Name a guardian plus a trustee to manage the money you leave behind.**

You also want to name beneficiaries (any person who receives the money if you die) on all your insurance policies and all your retirement accounts. This includes IRAs, 401(k) plans, 403(b) plans and any other investment account you might have.

Additionally, consider having a living will—also called an Advance Healthcare Directive. The legal document specifies the medical treatment you wish to receive in the event of a life-threatening injury, particularly if you suffer a coma or require life support. Living wills are available free on many websites. An excellent source is www.agingwithdignity.org.

Finally, establish powers of attorney, both a financial power of attorney and a healthcare power of attorney. The document allows someone you trust to sign legal documents on your behalf and manage situations that arise the way you would want to have them handled. For example, if you suffer a coma, your financial power of attorney could write checks on your checking account to pay your bills for you, while your medical power of attorney could instruct the doctors on your care management. Most attorneys offer powers of attorney and living wills for little or no additional fee when they write your will.

Financing College Education

In my opinion, individuals today are racking up too much debt in student loans—the amounts are crazy! The cost of private college is a significant factor in loans gone wild. Before deciding upon a college that is well above your means, be aware that top companies recruit from the top state schools as well. Many prestigious CEOs attended state schools. Strongly consider a state school for your child if you must borrow for tuition. In Georgia, the state pays tuition for students who maintain a certain grade point average. If this is available in your state, tell your child that you expect him or her to qualify for such scholarships. Also, make it perfectly clear to your kids that if they lose a scholarship from "partying too hardily," then they better have a backup plan for earning or borrowing the money for their tuition.

Certainly start saving for college the moment your children are born. Three percent of your gross income per year per child is a good rule of thumb, and save the money in a 529 college savings plan. Ask the grandparents to consider contributing to the 529 plan rather than buying expensive gifts for the children. College savings deliver far more benefit to your children in the long run!

Also keep in mind that you can borrow money for college, but you cannot borrow for retirement. If you must choose between the two, save for your own retirement and find other ways to handle college. Consider junior colleges and state schools. Require your child to take a lighter class load so that he or she has ample time for a job that will cover some or all of the expenses.

> **You can borrow money for college, but you can't borrow money for retirement. Funding your retirement comes before funding college for your children.**

When I discuss college with clients, parents wonder: Should they pay for their children's graduate school? My answer will depend on the family's financial situation. Your personal values also matter. Some parents believe their children should be responsible for their own graduate school expenses because the experience of earning their way is character building. Others believe an education is the most valuable gift they can ever give their children, and they want to provide that opportunity. Both are valid—make the choice that is right for you.

If money is a huge issue for college, consider alternative ways to pay for the education. One idea is having your child join ROTC (Reserve Officer Training Corps). Or your child could work for an employer willing to subsidize continued education. Also, in many professions, such as teaching and nursing, employers regularly agree to pay off college loans in exchange for a certain number of years of service.

While your children are in college, one of the biggest gifts you can give them is to monitor borrowing, both on student loans and on credit cards. Parents who remain focused on this matter give their children a tremendous gift of graduating with either no debt or as little debt as possible. Because many college students simply do not think through the ramifications of their spending while in college, assuming the role of benevolent dictator is a wise and loving move for any parent!

Monitor your child's debt while he or she is in college. This is a great time to be a benevolent dictator, preventing your child from getting over his or her head in debt.

If You'll Inherit

The manner in which you manage your money today is exactly how you are going to handle your inheritance. Adopt the habit of handling your money well right now so that when you inherit you will be able to hang on to it. The typical lottery winner in America is dead broke within seven years. People who inherit money tend to have similar outcomes.

Develop good money habits before you receive your inheritance. Let's recap the top wise habits: (1) have the right mental attitude, (2) stay out of debt, (3) save money every month, (4) have a written spending plan, (5) be adequately insured, (6) give some away to those in need, and (7) buy whatever you would like, so long as you pay cash.

Teach Your Kids about Money

As you create a solid financial path for yourself, you'll want to provide a roadmap for your children so that they can embrace the same smart practices. With certainty, I can tell you that the following are some of the most important actions to assume as parents:

1. Set a good example for your kids. They will learn much more from what you do than what you say.
2. Never waste money trying to keep up with the Joneses; teach your children how foolish that would be.
3. Give your children freedom to make choices with their money. The more you micromanage your children's handling of money, the less likely they are going to learn to do it well themselves. Give them some breathing room to make relatively small mistakes from which they can learn.
4. As your children earn money of their own, allow them plenty of freedom to spend that money while also teaching them how to be bargain shoppers.
5. Teach your children to save a minimum of 10% from everything they earn.
6. Let your children live with the consequences of their financial decisions. If you give them a weekly allowance on Sunday and they are broke on Tuesday, do not hand over extra cash. If they operate on a monthly budget yet spend their last dime by the 15th of the month, let them figure out how to get through the last two weeks of the month without a loan from you or your suggestions.
7. Teach your children the importance of staying out of debt. Of all my mother's financial lessons, this is the one for which I am most grateful to her.

8. Teach your kids to acquire as much education as they possibly can. Nothing raises income potential more than education.

9. Put saving for college on your priority list above a high level of gifts and extracurricular activities. Most families do not have enough money or time to do everything they would like. Therefore, make careful choices based upon benefiting your child's long-term future. Explain to your child how you have made your deliberate decisions.

10. The moment your children are born, begin saving three percent of your gross income per child per year for each one's college fund. I recommend a 529 college savings plan.

11. If you need to borrow money for college, tell your children that they must plan to attend a state school and teach them how to minimize the costs. Of course, if they receive a full scholarship to their top choice, accept it!

12. Teach your children that they can have anything their little hearts desire, just as long as they pay cash. Teach them to save first and spend second.

13. Teach your children to take good care of their health. Following healthy diets with proper exercise will prevent numerous medical problems—with exorbitant medical bills—in the future. Who wouldn't rather buy a vacation home than pay for heart surgery?

14. Teach your kids to be generous with others who are in need. Teach them to donate a certain percentage of their income on a regular basis. What goes around comes around, and givers receive amazing gifts in return.

15. Teach your children to pay their taxes honestly. Our country would fall apart if everyone attempted to "beat the system."

16. Teach them the importance of learning to handle their money well before they ever get married, as being in agreement about money is a key ingredient for a happy, harmonious marriage.

Things My Mom Said

After highlighting the fundamental financial lessons to teach your kids, I think this is a fitting place to relate some of my mother's favorite homilies. Feel free to repeat them as often as you like to your own children—and to yourself!

- Rich or poor, it is nice to have money.
- Money does not buy happiness, but I would rather be rich and miserable than poor and miserable.
- Don't do debt; *debt* is a nasty four-letter word.
- Paying interest is like throwing money out the window.
- If you cannot pay cash, you cannot afford it.
- It is not in the budget (she did not say we cannot afford it).
- You've got to have your union card (education).
- Only fools think the government will take care of them.
- Let someone else pay for all the depreciation on that new car.
- If you are big enough to quit school, you are big enough to live on your own. (We had no illusions that our mother would tolerate boomerang kids!)
- That is exactly what you get an allowance for (when we would beg our parents to buy us something at the store).
- Do not keep up with the Joneses; spend your money to create the life YOU want.
- You break it, you pay for it.
- If it seems too good to be true, it is too good to be true.
- Pay your bills on time and you will establish good credit.
- Plan ahead in case you live to be 100 years old.
- Do not invest your money until you have shopped around for the best options.

Final Words of Wisdom

Congratulations! If you have read this far, I know you are determined to handle your money well! Never forget that your mental attitude is the most critical ingredient in your recipe for creating wealth. I hope by now you are saying: *Yes, this is easy!*

If what I've just learned is all it takes to be rich some day, no problem!

> **I hope by now you are saying: Yes, this is easy! If what I've just learned is all it takes to be rich some day, no problem!**

If, in fact, it is your clear intention to be rich some day, you should find the critical steps are much easier to follow; similarly, saying *no* to the things that will knock you off track should be far less difficult. I have rarely been in debt since I was 24 years old. On the few occasions I have used debt, I have invariably prepaid the balance. I simply heard my mom's voice in the back of my head telling me that only dummies do debt, that paying interest is like throwing money out the window, that I can have anything I want so long as I pay cash. Keeping those ideals straight has helped me to remain operating on a cash basis.

I would not dream of *not* tracking my spending. I want to know every year how much my husband and I have saved and how much our net worth has increased. Over and over, I have seen that people who track their spending manage to save far more, and they are the same ones who find it easy to remain free of debt. If I happen to be feeling lazy, preferring not to bother with tracking my spending, I remind myself that winners do the things that losers don't like to do. I have always intended to be a big winner with my money, so I simply follow through!

Make up your mind—right this minute—you can and will follow these principles. Countless others have made the commitment and, as a result, they became rich.

> **Please send me an email at jan@GetYourAssets InGear.com to tell me about your progress.**

I'd love to hear from you! Please send me an email at jan@GetYourAssetsInGear.com to tell me about your progress. Also, let me know if you are still unclear about any areas or if you'd like for me to add more to certain topics in the future. Further, I encourage you to visit www.GetYourAssetsInGear.com, where you can take advantage of additional information. And do let me know of other training materials you'd like to see added to the site.

Now...*Get Your Assets in Gear!*

Action Step 14: Send me an email at jan@GetYour AssetsInGear.com to tell me about your progress.

Action Steps

Action Step 1: Take this quiz today, and then mark your calendar to take it again in a year to see how much progress you have made.

Action Step 2: Develop a positive attitude about money.

Action Step 3: Get out of debt and stay out of debt.

Action Step 4: Save 10% of your gross income for financial independence.

Action Step 5: Use a spending plan to track your money, to get out of debt, and to begin saving.

Action Step 6: Buy previously owned cars rather than new cars. Develop a plan so that you have the capability to pay cash for your cars.

Action Step 7: Keep your housing costs under 25% of your gross income, and pay off your mortgage before you retire.

Action Step 8: Do premarital financial planning and then work together to handle all of the necessary financial tasks.

Action Step 9: Trust that the universe and God are good; give money to charity with a cheerful, confident spirit.

Action Step 10: Be wise about investing by employing good asset allocation and good diversification.

Action Step 11: First determine your risk tolerance, then choose an appropriate asset allocation, then choose mutual funds to match this allocation plan.

Action Step 12: Earn a credit score of 700 or higher, and keep it there.

Action Step 13: Decide to follow what top achievers do in order to turbo charge the achievement of your goals.

Action Step 14: Send me an email at jan@GetYour AssetsInGear.com to tell me about your progress.

Helpful Resources

Authors of Interest
   www.Abraham-Hicks.com
   www.chellie.com
   www.briantracy.com
   www.ziglar.com

Brokerage companies
   www.tdameritrade.com
   www.etrade.com
   www.schwab.com
   www.scottrade.com

Budgeting
   www.mvelopes.com
   www.microsoft.com/money
   www.quicken.com
   www.personalfinancebudgeting.com

Credit
   www.annualcreditreport.com
   www.choicetrust.com
   www.myFICO.com
   www.equifax.com
   www.experian.com

www.transunion.com
www.consumer.gov/idtheft/
www.ftc.gov/bcp/conline/pubs/credit/repair.htm

Debt
www.DaveRamsey.com
www.cccsintl.org

General Personal Finance
www.bls.gov/oco – Occupational Outlook Handbook lists education requirements, earnings, and working conditions for thousands of jobs
www.bls.gov/bls/blswage.htm – Wages by area and occupation
www.FPAnet.org/public/tools/lifeevents – Education on everything from buying a home to marriage
www.consumerfed.org – Education on everything from protecting investments to buying cars
www.moneyhabitudes.com – Discover your true money habits and attitudes
www.hud.gov/buying – Important information about buying a home
www.fdic.gov/consumers/consumer/news/cnspr05

How to Find a Financial Planner
www.FPAnet.org
www.NAPFA.org

Investing
www.bigcharts.com
www.georgiainvests.org
www.morningstar.com
www.finance.yahoo.com

Living Wills
www.agingwithdignity.org/5wishes.html

Mutual Fund Companies
  www.vanguard.com
  www.fidelity.com
  www.troweprice.com

Saving
  www.EmigrantDirect.com
  www.eloan.com
  www.BankRate.com
  www.direct.citibank.com
  www.savingforcollege.com

Tax
  www.irs.gov

Please contact me at jan@getyourassetsingear.com to recommend additional websites to add to this list in future editions of this book.

About the Author

Jan Dahlin Geiger is a CERTIFIED FINANCIAL PLANNER™ practitioner with LongView Wealth Management in Atlanta, Georgia. Certified since 1988, she has helped hundreds of people turn their financial dreams into reality. For many years, Jan's instructional, inspirational seminars have been popular among civic groups, investment clubs, PTAs, churches, schools, and even prisons. Her diverse audiences are amazed to learn what Jan has long realized: that it is easy to get rich if you'll just follow a simple recipe and let it "bake" for many years.

Jan has appeared on a number of TV and radio programs, and has been quoted in *The Wall Street Journal, MSN Money, SmartMoney Magazine, Yahoo! Finance, The Chicago Tribune, MSNBC, Money Magazine, Reader's Digest, USA Today, the Atlanta Journal Constitution* and a host of other publications. She also appears frequently on Wedding Television Network's *Love and Money* show, on the *Living Life With Style With BB Webb* television show, and on the *Wall Street Chic* internet radio show.

Jan can be reached at:

LongView Wealth Management
1100 Johnson Ferry Rd., Suite 320
Atlanta, GA 30342-1743

404-843-3100
404-250-9850 (fax)

Corporate web page:
www.LongViewWealthManagement.com
Book web page: www.GetYourAssetsInGear.com

Special Offer for Investment Clubs and MasterMind Groups: Jan is happy to meet with your club or group by telephone conference call for 30 minutes when you buy 10 or more copies of her book. Please visit www.GetYourAssetsInGear.com to schedule Jan to speak with your group.

Printed in the United States
118818LV00002B/127-132/P